2000
Canadä

# Fintry:
## Loves, Lives and Dreams

The story of a unique Okanagan landmark

by
**Stan Sauerwein**
with
**Arthur Bailey**

Printed in Victoria, Canada

We acknowledge the financial support of the Government of Canada through the Canada Millennium Partnership Program for our publishing activities.

Cover design: Stan Sauerwein

**Canadian Cataloguing in Publication Data**

Sauerwein, Stanley.
    Fintry

    Includes bibliographical references.
    ISBN 1-55212-448-7

    1. Shorts Creek Delta (B.C.)--History.
I. Bailey, Arthur, 1929-   II. Title.
FC3845.S468S38 2000          971.1'5          C00-910972-2
F1089.S45S38 2000

# TRAFFORD

This book was published *on-demand* in cooperation with Trafford Publishing.
On-demand publishing is a unique process and service of making a book available for retail sale to the public taking advantage of on-demand manufacturing and Internet marketing.
**On-demand publishing** includes promotions, retail sales, manufacturing, order fulfilment, accounting and collecting royalties on behalf of the author.

Suite 6E, 2333 Government St., Victoria, B.C. V8T 4P4, CANADA
Phone       250-383-6864       Toll-free   1-888-232-4444 (Canada & US)
Fax         250-383-6804       E-mail      sales@trafford.com
Web site    www.trafford.com   TRAFFORD PUBLISHING IS A DIVISION OF TRAFFORD HOLDINGS LTD.
Trafford Catalogue #00-0113   www.trafford.com/robots/00-0113.html

10      9      8      7      6      5      4

For everyone who holds Fintry dear
and for all those who have yet
to find her
and dream.

# Contributing Donors

The authors wish to acknowledge the following for their financial contributions to this project's production. Without their foresight and willingness to assist, this history may have been lost to time. A portion of the revenue from each copy sold will be provided to the *Central Okanagan Heritage Society* as assistance in their ongoing restoration efforts.

**Canada Millennium Partnership Program**
**Central Okanagan Heritage Society**
**David Dawes**
**Sydney Dawes**
**Gary Erbacher**
**Susan Erbacher**
**Helen Graham**
**Peter Graham**
**William Graham**
**Ed Hall**
**Terry Hall**
**Investors Group**
**Glen K. Johnstone**
**Oli Johnstone**
**Bill Kennedy**
**Peter Kutney**
**Wendy McDonald**
**Paul Norris**
**Larry Salloum**

# Acknowledgements

There are many people to thank for their assistance in producing this book. The meaningful help of Central Okanagan Heritage Society providing services, and the financial aid received from the Canada Millennium Partnership Program, were both instrumental in moving this project from concept to book shelf. As important were the generous financial contributions received from all those people and organizations listed on the inside front cover.

We specifically wish to thank several individuals for their kind help, including Sandy Welbourn, past-president of the C.O.H.S. for his advice and encouragement and Senator Ross Fitzpatrick for his support of the objectives set for this project.

The task of writing would not have been as expeditious were it not been for the excellent prior research conducted and often published by the following groups and individuals: the membership of the Okanagan Historical Society, E.F. Digney, D.G. Falconer, David Dendy and others. Where it could be determined, specific research credits have been noted.

Of course, the new information uncovered would not have been included were it not for the willingness of descendents of the key players in Fintry's history to share their memories and heirlooms. We wish to thank the Menzies family particularly. We have been diligent in our efforts to present a true recollection of events, relationships and business dealings without personal judgements and thank everyone involved.

To the many, many people interviewed, we also offer our thanks. Art and Marie Harrop, Chrissie Stump, Janet Smith, Ingrid Bailey and Graham Bailey in particular. Thanks also to Ken Mather, the unflappable keystone of O'Keefe Historic Ranch, who always found time to sit down to talk, and who patiently provided research materials and advice.

Finally, thanks to Crystal Mandryk and David Hathaway for their advice and edit on the manuscript.

# Ingrid and Arthur Bailey

The longest residents and former owners, Arthur and Ingrid have devoted their lives to the preservation of the heritage at Fintry. Now that Fintry is a B.C. Provincial Park, the couple reside at Burnside enjoying the beauty of the area in their retirement.

# CONTENTS

May the best ye've ever seen
Be the worst ye'll ever see:
May a moose ne'er leave your pantry
Wi' a teardrap in his e'e.
May your lum keep bliethely reeking
Till you're auld enough tae dee,
May ye aye be jist as happy
As I wish ye aye tae be. *

*Taken from Fintry Christmas Card showing a picture of J.C.
Dun-Waters, the "Laird of Fintry" while hunting, circa 1930

# Introduction

*The Okanagan we know today was intensively sculpted by Ice Age events[1]. The Okanagan Lobe is described by geologists as the last advance of glacial ice in the Valley and they believe that it existed between 19,000 and 11,000 years ago[2]. The deglaciation of the area was largely completed by 9,000 years ago[3] but the main body of the valley remained choked with "stagnant ice" long after the surrounding land had thawed. As the last vestige of ice melted it created a gigantic waterway that stretched from Mara Lake, beyond Vernon, all the way south to MacIntyre Bluff near Vaseaux Lake[4]. The Okanagan Lake we enjoy boating on today is the surviving remnant.*

*Estimates of when man first found his way into this valley after the ice receded are imprecise. From various archeological site inventories done in the 1980s, the experts have determined that the Central Okanagan has been occupied for at least the past 4,000 years[5]. Archaeologist Mike Rousseau in fact, believes the First People arrived in the valley as long ago as 12, 000 to 11,000 BP (Before Present)[6]. So, it appears that ancestors of the Interior Salish may have enjoyed cultural continuity here from at least 9,000 years ago. How long that occupation actually included the area we call Fintry is anyone's guess.*

*The North Okanagan people who lived here (Okana'qen or Okanaqenix) are one of five groups within the Interior Salish linguistic family[7] and of the Okanagan-Colville Language Group[8]. Much like valley residents in mountainous regions elsewhere on earth, they seem to have communicated in a variety of dialects. Linguists have divided these early residents by language into two groups. The Okanagan: North Okanagan along the upper Okanagan; Similkameen Okanagan along the Similkameen River; Southern Okanagan along the lower Okanagan River; Methow Okanagan along the Methow River in Washington. And the Colville: Sanpoil-Nespelem along the Columbia River; Colville along the Colville Valley; and, Lakes along the Columbia River, Arrow Lakes and Slocan Lake.*

*As examples of the Interior Plateau peoples who occupied territory to the foothills of the Rockies, their culture was semi-sedentary. Louis Binford called the Okanagan "collectors"[9]. Their subsistence depended on hunting, fishing and gathering, he claimed. They would follow "a logical strategy where specific resources are exploited at different times by organized groups operating from base camps."*

*The Okanagan divided themselves into several distinct families and they maintained strong ties to that closely-knit structure, marking their place in the world by its very existence. Marriages for example, were seen as a service to the whole society rather than the individuals within it. Any Okanagan who, through carelessness or neglect, lost their status within the family were said to have 'lost their history'.*

*As fiercely independent individualists however, they didn't live in a hierarchical structure where one group followed the orders or others, except in special cases. The Okanagan made selections of a headman for special reasons only: They selected a chief of the hunt, for example; and, picked a chief for battle.*

*Each "band" traditionally resided in a large main village. How large their villages were depended on where plentiful seasonal food resources could be found. Pioneer ethnographer James Teit reported that the people living around Okanagan Lake were the "Upper" or "Lake" Okanagan and that two major bands occupied the area near Fintry with traditional villages to the north and south. The village at the north end of Okanagan Lake was known as Nkama'pElEks, which may be translated as "bottom, root, or neck end" of the lake. A village near Westbank, south of Fintry, was called StEkatElxEne'ut, translated as "lake on the side"[10].*

*On foot the families moved quite regularly up and down the valley in search of food, or to do their "collecting" as Binford described. They also wandered the valley for religious reasons[12].*

*The Interior Salish it appears, held strong beliefs in guardian spirit quests, in shamanism and spiritualism. At puberty, members would be required to leave the family and venture into the wilderness on vision quests. They sought known 'places of power', on a search to communicate with spirits they believed would guide them through their lives. Some of the successful, those with evident 'power' or sumix, might return to become healers or shaman. As a group, the First Peoples revered the land that sustained them and no doubt gave the Shorts Creek delta special significance because of its abundant animal life and edible plant life. In fact, descents of these aboriginal peoples still sincerely consider many areas along the western shore of Okanagan Lake to be repositories of special spiritual power. Some areas, particularly in and around the delta, are still reverently considered sacred by many of the descendants of these first valley residents.*

*Whatever their reasons for arriving, it was likely that they did so in the Spring and during the Fall. Low-elevation habitats like the lush delta were undoubtedly ideal locations for relaxed living. During the proper season, from places like the Shorts Creek delta, the Okanagan could hunt game and gather plant foods in nearby mid-elevation environments like the upper canyons around Fintry which they called Cougar Valley.*

*But what were they like? How did they do it? Thanks to the foresight of Native women like Louise Gabriel who took the time to record 'the old ways' in a published form, we have some small insight that we can be reasonably assured is an accurate snapshot.[13]*

*In a 1954 article in the Okanagan Historical Society annual report, Gabriel, with her friend Hester White, attempted to record some of the language and describe a little of the life of the First Peoples as it had been passed down through the generations through the Native aural tradition.*

*The "collecting" of course, occupied much of the First People's time. The Okanagan were adept hunters and used bows and arrows as their primary weapon.*

*Whether the men were hunting for deer, elk, mountain sheep, or grizzly bear they would have spent time on the delta in advance, preparing. They would have built themselves a sweat house beside the water on the delta flats and then under-*

*gone a cleansing ceremony. The object of the exercise was both spiritual and practical, but most likely the ritual was performed to ensure that their chosen prey would not catch their scent during the hunt. First Nations men in the North Okanagan still construct these sweat houses for special occasions such as gatherings before a marriage.*

*The sweat house was made with sticks embedded into the earth and bent towards the middle of a circle to form a small, round lodge. It was covered in bark and entirely packed with earth except for a small entrance draped with a skin or woven blanket. Inside, fir boughs were be spread around a small pit filled with hot rocks. The men would have stripped completely at the start of the ritual and then bathed in the cold nearby stream or the lake before entering the sweat lodge.*

*Inside, they underwent various prayer ceremonies calling for help and strength in the coming hunt from the 'unseen'. They rubbed themselves with clean grass to remove soil from their bodies and any callouses were carefully rubbed away with a smooth stone before the men emerged and once again bathed in the icy water of the creek or lake.*

*While the men hunted, the women gathered edible plants, the most important of which were balsamroot and bitterroot (Lewisa rediviva) which they dried and ground into flour, spring beauty (claytonia lanceolata), saskatoon berry and choke cherry[14]. Except for bitterroot, these same plants still survive in abundance in the Fintry area.*

*What the women foraged for and how it was prepared is as fascinating to understand as the men's pre-hunt ritual.*

*They gathered roots and cooked them before drying them in the sun. The roots they accumulated included the wild potato, the wild carrot, the tiger lily, and wild onions.*

*To prepare the roots, the women would dig a large pit and line it with hot rocks. Atop the rocks they would place the roots and then several layers of rose bush branches followed by a layer of timber grass and earth. Using water to create steam inside the structure, they would cook the roots overnight and then lay them out in the sun on tule mats to dry.*

*When the men returned to the delta base camp with their game, the women would be required to prepare the meat and hides while the hunters relaxed. The men would recount the highlights of the hunt, perhaps boast of their prowess, compete in foot and horse races or gamble with a stick game called lahal while the women worked.*

*Tanning the hides was a long process that involved skinning the animal and scraping the hide with a bone tool fashioned from the leg of a deer. Once completely scraped, the hide was stretched and dried in the sun, then smoked over a fire and finally soaked in warm water full of cooked animal brains.*

*Then the hide would be stretched to a frame again and beaten with a smooth rock in order to soften it. Once dry, it would be smoked one more time before being cut into pieces with a stone knife and turned into moccasins and clothes.*

*As a technologically primitive people, compared to the Europeans (sa-ma) who arrived in their midst along the shores of Okanagan Lake early in the 1800s, the Okanagan had few artifacts that might survive time. Their material culture was distinguished by tools of bone and antler, chipped or ground stone[15]. To carry their gatherings they wove baskets from reeds or fashioned birch bark containers. They slept on tule rush mats and sheltered themselves in summer along the banks of the river or lakeshore under temporary pole-and-tule mat structures called mat lodges.*

*So, it is not surprising that no conclusive evidence that these First People spent any time living at Fintry has ever been uncovered. It is most likely that they moved to sheltered wintering grounds near main waterways or fishing stations where they lived in distinctive semi-subterranean pithouses called kekuli.*

*In the 1950s, archaeological sites along the Westside Road were catalogued according to the Borden Site Designation Scheme[16]. This cataloguing scheme used throughout Canada and is based on maps of the National Topographic System. It uses latitude and longitude to pinpoint a site's location.*

*With the Borden scheme, four alternating upper and lower case letters (e.g., EaQu) are used to designate a unique 10 degree latitude (18.4 km north-south) by 10 degree longitude (11.2 km east-west) "block". Sites are numbered sequentially within a block usually based upon their date of discovery.*

*In the Central Okanagan, the first archaeological site survey was conducted in 1953 by Warren Caldwell. The University of Washington archaeologist recorded eight sites on the west side of Okanagan Lake from the Tsinstikeptum Indian Reserve #10 in Westbank to the Okanagan Indian Reserve #1 at Whiteman Creek. A more systematic inventory of prehistoric archaeological sites was conducted 23 years later along the shore of Okanagan Lake by Steven Lawhead and Kevin McAleese. As a result of their work in 1976, about 50 sites were recorded[17] including what appear to be some of Caldwell's sites re-recorded under a different number. Further study, mostly for development purposes, has resulted in that total now listing 68 prehistoric and historic archaeological heritage sites.*

*However, as previously stated, no "incontrovertible evidence" that the Shorts Creek delta was ever consistently used as a "base camp" for the First Peoples has ever been found.*

*Five archeological sites of apparent prehistoric antiquity at Fintry were recorded in the 1976 survey and revisited by archeologists in 1990[18].*

*A scatter of three basalt and two chalcedony waste flakes were found on a 50 m length of beach that extended east from the boat launch ramp and marina for example. The waste flakes would have been the 'garbage' evidence of manufacture of arrow heads for example. These materials were collected in 1976 but in 1990 archeologists could not relocate the area again and have been forced to regard its archeological significance as low.*

*Also in 1976, between the Manor and the Packing House archeologists found a small corner-notched arrow head and a retouched stone flake. Both were manufactured from basalt. One chert flake and one chalcedony flake were also found[19]. Another arrow head was discovered in 1990 and resulting excavations undertaken, but the lack of further evidence forced the archeologists to conclude this area, as well, was one of low significance.*

*If the First Peoples spent their summers and falls hunting on the delta for generations some evidence should logically have been apparent. The closest any studies were able to come to proof were vague ground depressions which might have been the remnants of a housepit (EaQv5) and a small rock shelter beneath a detached block of granodiorite near the toe of the mountain slope 375 m south of the boat launching ramp[20].*

*Another location, a shallow cave at EaQv4, offered another possibility for evidence however it gave up no un-equivocal proof to the 1976 survey team. The 1990 archeo-logical study that revisited the same site turned up only char-coal chunks and possible carbon staining on the roof of what may have been a shelter. It has to be concluded that this site, now very near the new expanded network of B.C. Parks camp-sites, may never have been a shelter at all.*

*When faced with this dearth of evidence that the Okanagan were anything more than occasional visitors to the delta, modern descendants only smile. The proof, they say, cannot be seen with the eyes. Aural history passed from generation to generation among the Natives living between Vernon and Kelowna claims Terrace Mountain, located north of Short's Creek, was known to the local Indians by the game commonly found there - Big Horn Sheep[21]. Variously, the name has been recorded as Illiquilliken [22], La-te-kwil-e-ten and Kee-le-kwil-tin.*

*The Indian name for the Shorts Creek delta however is not definitive and some confusion exists, as the Indian appella-tion given it was also applied to a village that existed in more recent memory located about three kilometers north of Siwash Creek at the head of the Lake. Recorded references to the local Indian place name for the delta exist as Sinquina Otiaton [23] which is translated as 'Jump on their backs'; Sinquinatiaton translated as 'Ambush by Rival'; Sinkohotem [24] translated as 'Massacred'; Sinkohoton; SntlEmuxte'n [25] translated as 'Place where slaughtered'; and, Sin-kina-ot-iat [26] translated as 'Massacred'. The Shuswap name for Shorts Creek is recorded as Nikwin-i-atin [27] translated as 'Where the female red deer are caught'.*

*Some of the Indian names have a common reference to a series of ongoing territorial battles that went on between the Okanagan Indians and the Shuswaps until about 1700[28].*

*One version of that story claims an Okanagan war party*

*ambushed between three and four hundred Shuswap warriors camped at the base of the cliffs on the delta and killed them by causing a rockslide[29]. However, as previously indicated, archeological surveys found no evidence of such a massacre in the form of bones or skeletons. Did it really happen? At this point it is only a story.*

*The watershed area of Short's Creek was also known as Myars-kala, the place of the little men — Inchama skylugh [30].*

*According to the Native aural history, the delta area was occupied by aggressive 'little men' who were well known and feared by Native populations as far as the Shuswap (who called them Tsu-in-i-tem). The verbal history claims these residents, though only two feet tall, were skilled hunters and powerful. As fierce protectors of their territory, the legends claim the Tsu-in-i-tem watched the area from a cave in the mountainside above Nahun and would attack intruders by leaping onto their backs and breaking their necks. Recent inquiry into the subject of the Tsu-in-i-tem with descendents of the First Peoples indicates a deeper meaning to these stories. They may in fact be the essence of cultural myths that the Natives hold sacred... and secret.*

# Introduction Notes

1   Arcas Consulting Archaeologists Ltd., *Archaeological Impact Assessment, D.L. 686 and D.L. 2920 At Fintry, Near Kelowna, BC*

2   Kershaw, A.C., *The Quaternary history of the Okanagan. Forty-second Annual Report of the Okanagan Historical Society*: pp 27-42. 1978

3   Fulton, R.J., *G.S.C. Memoir 380*. Quaternary geology and geomorphology, Nicola-Vernon area, British Colum bia. Ottawa. 1975

4   Kershaw, A.C., *The Quaternary history of the Okanagan. Forty-second Annual Report of the Okanagan Historical Society*: pp 27-42. 1978

5   Arcas Consulting Archaeologists Ltd., *Archaeological Impact Assessment, D.L. 686 and D.L. 2920 At Fintry, Near Kelowna, BC*

6   M. Rousseau, *BC Studies*, No. 99,: p 140. Autumn 1993

7   Teit, J.A., The Salishan tribes of the western plateaus: the Okanagon. In *Annual Reports of the Bureau of Ameri can Ethnology* 45: pp 198-294. Washington, D.C. 1930

8   F.M. Buckland, *Ogopogo's Vigil - A History of Kelowna and the Okanagan*: p 6. Okanagan Historical Society. 1948

9   J. Webber, En'Owkin Centre, *OK Sources*: pp 54-89. Theytus Books, Penticton, 1990

10  Ray, V.F., *Cultural Relations in the Plateau of North western America*. Publications of the Frederick Webb Hodge Anniversary Publication Fund, Volume III. Los Angeles. 1939

11  L. Gabriel and H.E. White, *Food and Medicines of the Okanakanes*, Okanagan Historical Society Report No. 18: pp 24-29. 1954

12  *OK Sources*, p 30.

13  L. Gabriel and H.E. White, *Food and Medicines of the Okanakanes*, Okanagan Historical Society Report No. 18: pp 24-29. 1954

14  Turner, N.J., Bouchard, R., and D.I.D. Kennedy, *Ethnobotany of the Okanagan - Colville Indians of Brit ish Columbia and Washington*. British Columbia Pro

vincial Museum, Occasional Paper Series No. 21. Victoria.
1980

15   Arcas Consulting Archeologists, *Heritage Sites Overview*. 1992

16   Borden, C.E., *Anthropology in British Columbia* 3: A uniform site designation scheme for Canada pp 44-48. Victoria. 1952

17   Lawhead, S., and McAleese, K., *Interior Lakes Archaeological Inventory (Okanagan Lake Survey: 1976)*. Report on file, Minis try Library, Ministry of Tourism and Ministry Responsible for Culture, Victoria. 1976

18   Arcas Consulting Archeologists Ltd., *Archaeological Impact Assessment, D.L. 686 and D.L. 2920 At Fintry, Near Kelowna, BC;* Consultant's report on file, Ministry Library, Ministry of Tourism and Ministry Responsible for Culture. 1990

19   ibid

20   Digney, E.F., Notes for a Fintry history compiled from various sources. 1983

21   Real Estate Review, *Indian Place Names*. Sept 10 issue, p 16. 1987

22   ibid

23   Digney, E.F., Notes for a Fintry history compiled from various sources. 1983

24   Teit, J.A., The Salishan tribes of the western plateaus: the Okanagon. In *Annual Reports of the Bureau of American Eth nology* 45: pp 198-294. Washington, D.C. 1930

25   Ormsby, M.A., British Columbia, A History. 1958

26   Digney, E.F., Notes for a Fintry history compiled from various sources. 1983

27   ibid

28   Real Estate Review, *Indian Place Names*. Sept 10 issue, p 16. 1987

29   Digney, E.F., Notes for a Fintry history compiled from various sources. 1983

30   ibid

# CHAPTER 1
## THE 'SA-MA' TRAVEL THROUGH

The first European exploration of the Okanagan was done in 1811 by Scottish traders the Natives called 'Sa-ma'.

From their first glimpse of the valley through the two decades that followed, the Okanagan was a way-point on an important inland trading route that penetrated western North America from the shores of the Columbia River, to the northern remoteness of Fort St. James.

The race between British and Americans to capitalize on the fur bounty in western North America had already been raging for many years. From 1670, with Charles II's charter and the incorporation of the Hudson's Bay Company, men with adventurous and sometimes avaricious spirits had been slowly crossing the northern latitudes of Canada in search of pelts.

Another company, the North West Fur Company, held sway over a vast trading area of wintry lakes and boundless forests in Canada's hinterland that the HBC hadn't reached. Furs and skins were also casually being collected by the country traders in the United States and New Yorker John Jacob Astor, the richest man in America, was one of them.

Sensing a vast potential for profit in the Pacific Northwest, Astor 'cut a deal' with the Nor'Westers to share in his fur trading profits if they left his traders unmolested.

He outfitted one of his ships, the Tonquin, and hired an unruly band of Canadian voyageurs, trappers and adventurers to conduct trade on his behalf. They included Alexander McKay, Duncan McDougal , David and Robert Stuart, and twelve clerks and apprentices including Alexander Ross, Francis Pillette, Donald McLean and Ovid de Montigny[1].

19

On a fresh southwest wind on the morning of September 8, 1810 the Tonquin set sail for the Columbia River out of New York Harbour. It took six-and-a-half months, until March 22, 1811, to land the Tonquin at the mouth of the Columbia. A suitable location for a trading post was selected several miles upstream, goods offloaded and on April 11, 1811 John Jacob Astor's western enterprise was born. The traders called it Fort Astoria.

On July 23 David Stuart set out with Pillet, Ross, McLennon and Montigny, two voyageurs and two Sandwich Islanders to begin trading. They had three canoes laden with everything they needed to set up a post in the Interior.

Alexander Ross. *Image courtesy Okanagan Historical Society*

At the junction of the Oakinacken River and the Columbia, not far from the present community of Brewster, Washington they established their first post. The Indians told Stuart the Oakinacken had its source "in a considerable lake about 150 miles west of the point of the junction"[2] Stuart and company adopted the Native name for the place, calling the post Fort Oakinacken.

Just a few days after establishing a post that would become a critical link to Pacific Fur Company's trading, David Stuart made a decision. While the area selected for Fort Oakinachen was commodious and could sustain a large post, they'd arrived too late in the season to construct a fort that would shelter their party, even under subsistence conditions. He also knew the Astorians had to push further into the territories in face of the Nor'Wester's activity, so he decided to split his group.

For safety's sake he sent half of the party, Pillet and McLean with two voyageurs, back to Astoria[3]. He kept Ross, Montigny and two others with him at Fort Oakinachen and on September 16[4] he and Ovid Montigny set out to travel north. A few days earlier, they'd met a large group of South Okanogan Indians, led by Chief Sopa, and found them to be friendly and willing to trade. Stuart had purchased four horses from Sopa, and he received two more as gifts from the Chief. In trade for each horse, he

Fort Oakinachen was located at the junction of the Columbia and the Okanogan Rivers. *Image courtesy of the Okanagan Historical Society.*

gave Sopa a yard of printed cloth and two yards of red gartering.[5] They planned a short journey along the river and then onwards along the lake previously described by the Indians.

It's likely that once they reached the Okanagan Valley they continued onward because the countryside did not offer an environment suitable for the fur-bearing animals that the traders sought[6]. Ross's own recollections[7] fail to describe the passage through the area we know as Fintry.

"After leaving this place, we bent our course up the Oak-in-ach-en, due North for upwards of 250 miles till we reached its source. Then crossing a height of land, fell upon Thompson's River, after travelling for some time among the powerful Nation called the She-waps."

Stuart settled at the junction of the North and South Thompson Rivers at "Cumloups", a location that they would soon rename Kamloops. The Indians there had already been canvassed by a Kootenay named Pila-ka-lah-uh for trade with the Nor'Westers, so Stuart would have been pleased to find the "She-waps" amenable to barter.

He describes the time spent there as most pleasant: "The snow fell while we were in the mountains, and prevented our immediate return. After waiting for fine weather the snow got so deep that we considered it hopeless to attempt getting back, and therefore passed the time with the She-waps and other tribes in that quarter. The Indians were numerous and well-disposed, and the country throughout abounded in beavers and all kinds of fur, and I have made arrangements to establish a Trading Post

21

there in the ensuing Winter. On the 26th of February we began our home-ward journey and spent just twenty-five days on our way back. The distance may be about 280 miles (460 km)."[8]

The return journey took Stuart until March 22. In all, his little investigative trip took him 188 days. A month later, with the protection of some of Astoria's men who'd come up the Columbia to Fort Oakinachen with food and merchandise that Spring, Stuart started for Astoria bearing the first shipment of furs to pass by Fintry. His shipment of 2,500 beaver skins "worth in our money at that time $7.50 each on the Canton market in China, where they would be sold. These skins cost the traders about 12 cents a piece in merchandising."[9]

Evidence of the rich opportunities in furs to the North must have excited Ross, who'd been left in charge of Fort Oakinachen. On May 16, after being relieved of responsibility for their first Interior trading post, it was Ross' turn to take the journey. With his clerk Boullard, an unidentified Indian and 16 saddle and pack horses he returned to the land of the 'She-waps'. It is not known what precise route he took to reach Kamloops, but undoubtedly he made frequent use of the Indian tracks that lay on the west side of Okanagan Lake as well.

It took Ross, loaded down with furs, until July 12 to return to the Columbia River, just in time to say goodbye to Stuart who had prepared to leave in August with a fresh stock of trading goods necessary to establish a permanent Kamloops trading post. Again, the train of animals would have passed along the lake and probably rested for a time at Fintry.

The men passed the winter in peace and lucrative trade, but the following year the War of 1812 forced the Astorians to sell all their furs and trading goods to representatives of the Nor'Westers.

The purchase effectively opened an alternative Nor'Wester supply route to New Caledonia from the Pacific via the Columbia River. For the remainder of 1813 and for all of 1814, New Caledonia relied on Fort Astoria (quickly named Fort George by the Canadians after the purchase) for supplies. The following two years saw supplies flowing from Montreal, but the insanity of that business decision became obvious to Company directors quickly. By 1816, the supply route from the Columbia, travelling past Fintry, was again primary.

Competition for the furs continued without pause along the west coast. Through the five years that followed, the Hudson's Bay Company became the most powerful trading force across the entire north of the continent. Inevitably in 1821, because of the Hudson's Bay Company's growing influence, the Nor'Westers were swallowed by their competition.

Nonetheless, the Okanagan Fur Brigade Trail continued to be used

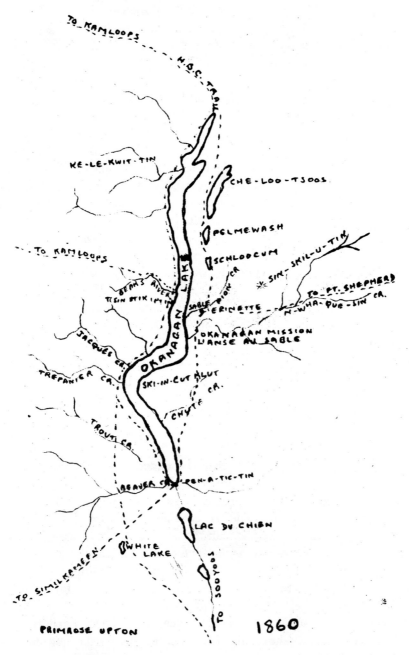

This map, produced by Frank Buckland, illustrates the Native place names given to various areas of the Okanagan at about the time of the Ross expedition. *Image courtesy of the Okanagan Historical Society.*

as the supply route for New Caledonia until 1823 when the Hudson's Bay Company, much like the Nor'Westers before them, thought they had a better idea. For a two year period of what was undoubtedly economic lunacy, the Hudson's Bay Company supplied New Caledonia from their post of York Factory on Hudson Bay.

Though supplies were not coming up the trail, furs were being transported down. In 1825, William Connolly took a load of furs from New Caledonia to Fort Vancouver via the overland route. Historians therefore mark this as the true institution of the Hudson's Bay Fur Brigade Trail despite the preceeding history proving otherwise.[10] By 1826, Sir George Simpson, the Governor, decided on this overland route making more sense than supply caravans travelling from eastern Canada and the Columbia supply point was again pressed into service. Simpson moved the anchor for the route from Fort George to a new post called Fort Vancouver, almost 100 miles upstream on the north bank of the Columbia.

For two decades following, the trail through the Okanagan was used to carry provisions and trading goods to Kamloops and New Caledonia and then to transport back the furs. Every winter until 1847, the furs that had been traded at the posts were gathered. In April, fur goods from Fort St. James, Fort Fraser, Fort McLeod and Fort George started down the Fraser Fiver to Fort Alexandria, south of what is now Quesnel.

From Alexandria, horse trains plodded in single file past Fintry enroute to Fort Okanogan where the traders would rendezvous with others from New Caledonia, the Thompson and Colville. Together, in one large group, they would proceed by boat down the Columbia River to Fort Vancouver sometime in June.[11]

In all, the transport of the furs from the wilderness to Fort Vancouver would take two months from first departure at Stuart Lake. Then, after a month-long rest while supplies were gathered, the 20-day return trip to Fort Okanogan would begin. The groups would split into their separate directions from there and start the process anew. Usually, the trip from Fort Vancouver to Fort St. James took two months.

Reports show that as many as 300 horses made up the brigades that travelled from Fort Okanogan to Fort Alexandria. A split load of 168 pounds was assigned each horse. The journey though long, was taken rather casually by the traders after so many years of practice. Each day of the trek would begin at the civilized hour of nine or ten in the morning and halt by three or four in the afternoon. An average day's distance was only 20 miles, and even that could vary depending on the difficulty of the terrain being crossed.

When The Oregon Treaty of 1846 designated the 49th parallel as boundary between British and American territory, it forced abandonment of the Okanagan Fur Brigade Trail as a supply route for commercial reasons. If the Hudson's Bay Company wished to supply their posts from the Pacific at Fort Vancouver, they would be required to pay the American government a duty on crossing this new border. To the HBC, that kind of tax was unthinkable. The final brigade passed through the Okanagan Valley in 1847. Alternatively a year later, the brigades from New Calendonia transported furs over the Cascade Mountains from Fort Kamloops to Yale, but many of the 400 horses gathered for the journey were unbroken and the footing on the way so treacherous a large number were lost to the swirling torrents of the Fraser River. Because of the losses, then Governor Douglas decided another route called Anderson's Trail had to be used from Fort Kamloops through the Coquihalla River Valley. A new depot was constructed for that purpose at a place called Fort Hope. In 1849 the barely passable Hope Trail was used for the first time.[12]

For 12 years after the last HBC brigade passed through, the trail returned to its origins and was travelled only by the Indians living along the shores of Okanagan Lake. Then in 1858, with the discovery of gold in the Cariboo, the trail was again revived because of its convenience by miners and cattlemen who cared less about international agreements than toiling for gold or feeding the men who did.[13]

# Chapter One Notes

1   F.M. Buckland, *Ogopogo's Vigil - A History of Kelowna and the Okanagan*: p 7. Okanagan Historical Society. 1948
2   ibid p 2
3   Irving, W., *Anecdotes of an Enterprise Beyond the Rocky Mountains*: p 67
4   F.M. Buckland, *Ogopogo's Vigil - A History of Kelowna and the Okanagan*: p 6. Okanagan Historical Society. 1948
5   ibid:p 6
6   Ormsby, M.A., *British Columbia, A History*. 1958
7   Ross, A, *Fur Hunters of the Far West*. 1810-1813
8   F.M. Buckland, *Ogopogo's Vigil - A History of Kelowna and the Okanagan*: p 6. Okanagan Historical Society. 1948
9   ibid: p 7
10  Ormsby, M. A., *The Significance of the Hudson's Bay Brigade Trail*. Okanagan Historical Society. Thirteenth Report: 1904
11  ibid
12  Ormsby, M.A., *British Columbia, A History*. 1958
13  Ormsby, M. A., *The Significance of the Hudson's Bay Brigade Trail*. Okanagan Historical Society. Thirteenth Report: 1904

# CHAPTER TWO
# THE FUR BRIGADE TRAIL

If the track along Lake Okanagan had not existed, if the European traders had been forced to find a different route to move their trade goods inland and the furs they gathered back to the Pacific, perhaps settlement of this valley by Whitemen might have taken a different course. It would definitely have altered recent Native history. Hwistesmetxeqen, 'Walking Grizzly Bear' for example, may not have become one of the greatest chiefs in the memory of the Okanagan people.

At least two generations before the first Whitemen cast a covetous eye on his valley, Hwistesmetxeqen's great-grandfather Pelkamulox, 'Rolls-over-the-earth', settled near the junction of the Okanagan and Similkameen Rivers[1].

During his lifetime, Pelkamulox employed an Indian form of diplomacy to guarantee the safety of his people. He married into the families of his enemies. He had four wives; a Spokan, a Shuswap, a Sanpoil and an Okanagan. These various unions resulted in an undetermined number of offspring, but four of them were known to have become chiefs. One, Kwolila, eventually became chief of the Kamloops band of the Shuswap tribe. Another, also named Pelkamulox, was Hwistesmetxeqen's father and hereditary chief of the Okanagan.

This third generation Pelkamulox was one of the first Okanagan natives to meet Whitemen.

He was aggressive and territorial, spending much of his time repelling invaders from the stone fortifications he built at a place the Natives called Salilx, 'Heaped-up-stone-house' near the junction of the rivers he called home. After a particularly dangerous season of attacks, Kwolila, fearing for his half-brother's safety, convinced the Okanagan chief to move north to a tract of land he was willing to give him near Kamloops.

Pelkamulox and his band settled at Fish Lake in an area that later became known as the Nicola country. There under the wing of his half-brother, he discovered the peace and safety that his grand-father had enjoyed through marriage. Pelkamulox's people spent their summers roaming the plateau down to the Fintry delta and their winters at the village of Nkama'peleks, near the head of Lake Okanagan north of Fintry. As a result of his move, Pelkamulox had free time and he devoted much of it traveling to the scattered Indian nations surrounding his territory. He became familiar with the Shuswap, Sanpoil, Coeur d'Alene, Nez Perce, Spokan, Kutenai, and Shoshone. Pelkamulox lived up to his name. On occasion he even ventured beyond the Rockies on bison hunting expeditions. It was on one such trip that he met Whitemen for the first time.

The Whites, likely employees of the Nor'Westers, intrigued him with their looks and fearsome weapons. He befriended these strangers and observed them as a modern reporter might. On his return to the Okanagan, he spoke of them to anyone who would listen. His tale of men with faces the color of snow built him an enviable reputation as a story-teller. So famous did he become among the various tribes in fact, he was invited by the Shuswap to visit a village called Hah-ilp at the foot of Pavilion Mountain on the Fraser River to describe his encounter.

Not everyone he met believed his wild reports. During his story-telling tour with the Fountain Band of the Lillooet tribe, one chief took exception.

According to a generally accepted version[2] of the story:

"A chief from Seton Lake arose and advised the people to pay no more attention to these stories. The chief went on to say that what they had heard was false; that there were no human beings who had white skins, blue eyes, and light, short, curly hair, who covered themselves with woven material which kept them warm without encumbering their movements; that there was no weapon with which birds could be killed in their flight; that there were no shoes with which one could walk over cactus without being pricked, nor any such thing as a metal tube by which animals could be killed at a distance equal to the width of the Fraser; that no missile could be projected so fast that the eye could not follow it; and, that there was no weapon that made a noise like thunder and at the same time produced smoke like fire. He further denied that there was any animal on which men could ride safely and be carried faster than the swiftest buffalo. He said, in fact, that Pelkamulox was a liar and should not be listened to by men and warriors."

The rebuke was an unforgivable insult that set the stage for Hwistesmetxeqen's future. On hearing the insult, Pelkamulox is said to have reached for his bow. Before he could draw an arrow from his quiver he was shot twice by the Lillooet chief.

Mortally wounded, Pelkamulox was carried back to the Shuswap camp where, as he was dying, he begged his half-brother Kwolila to assume the guardianship of his son, Hwistesmetxeqen. More importantly, he got Kwolila to agree to help Hwistesmetxeqen someday avenge his death.

With Pelkamulox's passing, the leadership of the Okanagan tribe moved to 'Walking Grizzly Bear'. A young chief, Hwistesmetxeqen, or Nkwala as he was also known, lived with a growing hatred for the treacherous Lillooet. It was years however before he could see a way to get revenge for his father's murder. Whitemen, it turned out, were the deliverance of his satisfaction.

Following Stuart's first historic trip inland through Fintry, Ovid Montigny was dispatched to establish a small trading post at the north end of the lake near the native village of Nkama'peleks. Montigny, with another French Canadian named Pion, became friends with Nkwala. After the first successful winter of trading, Montigny and Pion returned to the Columbia leaving their trade goods at Nkama'peleks in the charge of Nkwala.

With the theft they'd experienced dealing amongst other tribes, when Montigny returned to the Nkama'peleks village months later and found all his goods still safe, he was overjoyed. In gratitude, he rewarded Nkwala with 10 rifles, ammunition, tobacco and vermilion.

That winter Nkwala left his warriors training with the firearms at Nkama'peleks while he travelled to Walla Walla. At the time of his father's death, horses had been unknown to many of the Interior Indians, which was why the Lillooet chief had scoffed at Pelkamulox's story, but Nkwala knew the Whites had horses. Nkwala bartered furs at Walla Walla for a horse and returned to Nkama'peleks after several months, ready to seek his revenge.

The following year he implored the Shuswap, Thompson and Similkameen tribes to join him in a war on the powerful Lillooets. Waiting until late summer for the height of the salmon run, Nkwala led a band of 500 warriors. He swept through the Lillooet country in a sudden and ferocious attack, his warriors firing their weapons while he commanded them from the back of his huge horse. By the time the attacks were over, 300 Lillooet had been killed, many taken as slaves, and Nkwala had finally proven his father's story was true.

Nkwala's power as the great chief of the Okanagan grew through the ensuing years and the changing face of trading as the Pacific Fur Company was swallowed by the Nor'Westers and then by the Hudson's Bay Company. In part at least, his rise to power was spawned by the interaction he had with the white traders along the trail that snaked through his territory.

By 1846, 'Nicola' as he was now known by the Whites, was the most powerful Indian chief in the entire North West. The 1849 Alexander Caulfield Anderson map of the North West is evidence of the regard in which Nicola was held by both his people and the White traders. In unusual deference to an Indian, the map shows 'Nicola's River' and 'Nicola's Country' as designated landmarks. In the vast interior territory he commanded, he also had a lake, a plateau and a valley named after him and he was the overlord of thousands of square miles through which the Whitemen travelled from the Columbia to Kamloops. Even when the Oregon Treaty set the 49th parallel as the boundary between Canada and the United States and split Nicola's nation in half it meant nothing to his people. While Nicola chose to live on the 'Queen's Side' from that day forward, he remained as 'head chief' to Okanagan Indians in both the U.S. and Canada[3] until his death in 1865 and men travelled the trail in peace with his blessing. In fact, he may have even encouraged it. Under Nicola, the Okanagans cultivated patches of corn, potatoes and even tobacco. He had large bands of horses and may have himself acquired cattle from the first recorded cattle drive along the old Fur Brigade Trail.

The first cattle drive was organized the year of the border settlement by General Joel Palmer and consisted of cattle and several wagons[4]. The number and size of the herds abruptly stopped when the U.S. government imposed an embargo on cattle export as a Civil War measure in late 1862. Later, at least 1868, cattle were driven from Oregon to the Cariboo and Big Bend (Columbia River gold fields) along the old Trail. Probably in the midst of just such a cattle drive in 1867, three partners — Cornelius O'Keefe, Thomas Wood and Thomas Greenhow — pre-empted the O'Keefe Ranch site at the head of Okanagan Lake[5]. Through the 1860s other routes were established to small settlements in the province's interior and the Okanagan Fur Brigade Trail was finally ignored again by all but the Natives living in the area.

Today, time has had its effect on the Okanagan Fur Brigade Trail. Cultivation, development, logging, landslides and new growth have obliterated the Trail in many spots.

Near Fintry, visitors can still walk in the footsteps of the traders, miners and settlers in various locations however thanks to the efforts of a

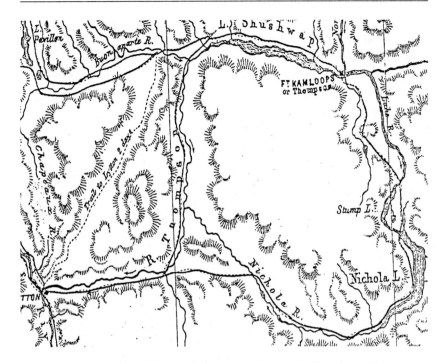

A map drawn by Lieutenants Palmer and Mayne of the Royal Navy and Royal Engineers in 1859, depicts part of Nikula's territory. This section shows the location of Fort Kamloops, the Fraser and the Thompson Rivers.

small group of members in the Okanagan Historical Society.

Beginning in 1974 a major effort to retrace the Trail and mark its location was begun by R.G. Harris of West Vancouver and H.R. Hatfield of Penticton, who believed a sizeable portion of the Westside Road is located on the old Trail. Their work was picked up by dedicated members of the Vernon Branch of the Society whose retracement efforts consisted of searching and identifing parts of the track that were still intact. The effort was fraught with difficulty and contention as private landowners along the route denied the Society access or argued the validity of their route determinations. Where it was clearly evident, the Society marked the Trail by nailing rectangular pieces of white metal to the trees or affixing occasional "HBC Trail" aluminum markers.

A more complete examination of the Trail's location can be found in a small document produced by the Vernon Branch of the Society in 1986 from which some of the above detail was gleaned. As well, original pre-emption survey maps and highway records seem to support the con-

31

tention that the present Westside Road was constructed over the old Fur Brigade Trail. In 1996 the Regional District of the Central Okanagan supported a recommendation by their Parks Advisory Committee that suggested the Westside Road be generally considered the location of the Trail even though another very well used trail, converted into the "Attenborough Road" crosses the "High Farm" above Fintry[6].

The Historical Society's determination of the Trail is generally considered the correct one therefore. To make identification of the Trail's location easier for casual hikers, the Society meticulously measured the track's distance from the junction of Westside Road and Highway 97 as a starting point.

Above Fintry, the Society's survey said that the Trail can be found at km 27.6 near the old original access road that winds from the Westside Road down to the delta. It is interesting to note that maps of the area made late in the 1800s name Shorts Creek Riviere a la Biche or Doe Creek[7] but earlier maps made in the late 1820s and early 1830s indicate no awareness of the delta in reference to the Fur Brigade Trail. This might indicate that the trail actually passed much higher to the West (perhaps the "High Farm" route), so far away in fact, that the delta could not be seen[8]. Nonetheless, a trail is found at the north side of this dirt road and runs relatively close to the Westside Road, passing through brush before emerging in a clearing. Several other trails, interwoven over the hillside also exist at this spot which tends to disguise the Trail, but the Society has maintained that the Trail ran parallel to the road.

The Trail they have marked winds down into an area of dense brush and reaches the end of its drop at about km 28.6 where the main branch of the Trail passes within 160 meters of a spring and the remnants of a cattle corral on the west side of the road.

Okanagan Historical Society documentation proposes that this corral area is likely the spot used by Northwest Botanist David Douglas, thought to have camped there on April 24, 1833.[9] Douglas, who was collecting specimens and taking astronomical observations and making a map of the country, was accompanying a Hudson's Bay Company "cattle party".

"This site would have been an excellent place for stock to feed and water and, at the time, the only one of its kind in the area," the authors of "The Okanagan Brigade Trail" propose.[10]

The corral mentioned is not visible from the Trail, but can be reached by hiking upwards through dense foliage. A spur of the Trail also leads up to the corral area if you are lucky enough to identify its location. "From the corral the trail leads north toward the Fintry Delta or south to where the dirt road is located," says the pamphlet.[11]

Much of the remaining evidence of this section of the Trail extending to the south of the Fintry Flat is overgrown and difficult to identify. Following the specific directions in the pamphlet is advised.

"The trail continues through a thickly forested area and although it is marked, attention must be paid so as not to lose sight of its course through the woods.

"Emerging from this densely wooded location, the trail climbs the hillside and then leads into a drier area where it becomes easier to follow. From here the trail turns directly into a subdivided area and is lost."[12]

The Fintry Delta section of the Trail is best reached from an old road that leaves Westside Road about 0.5 km north of Shorts Creek. The Trail drops in a series of switchbacks and begins again at the last switchback before the delta and can be traced northerly for about 1.5 km.

"The first part is a steady climb leading to a talus slope where the trail is obvious. From there the trail heads off, going through a park-like setting in the pine and fir forest, and providing a sweeping and attractive view of Okanagan Lake."[13]

Along the Trail from km 0.0 to Westwold, there are several locations where hikers can observe the remnants of Indian pictographs. This primitive art, believed to be considered sacred by members of the Westbank First Nation, has in some cases been identified as unique.[14] The nearest southerly pictograph is near Nahun. Originally reported in 1968[15] with provincial registration number EaQu1, it was on the Fur Brigade Trail about 150m west-northwest of the Nahun Wharf. It provides a definite visual link with the Fur Brigade Trail. The figures in the pictograph have been painted in red ochre on a granite rock face and are severely weathered. The portion painted on a white quartz vein however, is still visible and shows a row of "tally marks" flanked by two lifelike figures (perhaps a quadruped and a person).

The second, north of Fintry, is located on private property near the Okanagan Lake Forest Service Recreation Site, close to the lake shore and south of Indian Reserve #1. Because of its location and the fact access has been restricted by the property owner, this pictograph is fairly well preserved but difficult to find. It is one of the few examples of Interior Salish pictographs painted in a manner that superimposes images.

To view these pictographs, one must obtain permission from the property owner. The path worn to the Fur Brigade Trail is obvious in this area and quite visible. Travel to the junction of Bouleau Lake Road and Westside Road. In the Okanagan Lake Recreation Site, the Fur Brigade Trail leads away from the most southerly tip of the campground and winds through sparse ground cover following the lake. It climbs gradually to

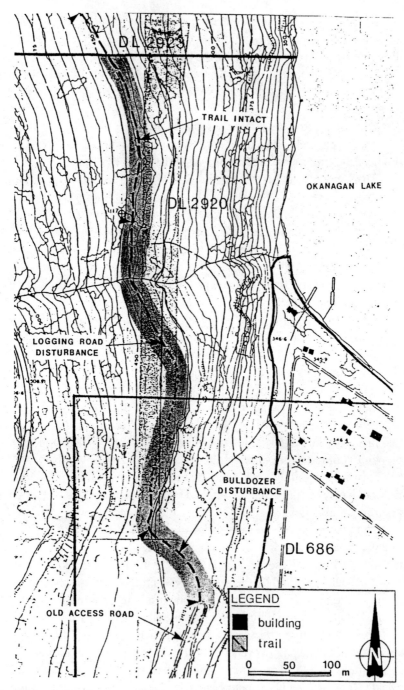

Fur Brigade Trail in the vacinity of Fintry circa 1990. *Image courtesy of Arcas Consulting Archaeologists Ltd.*

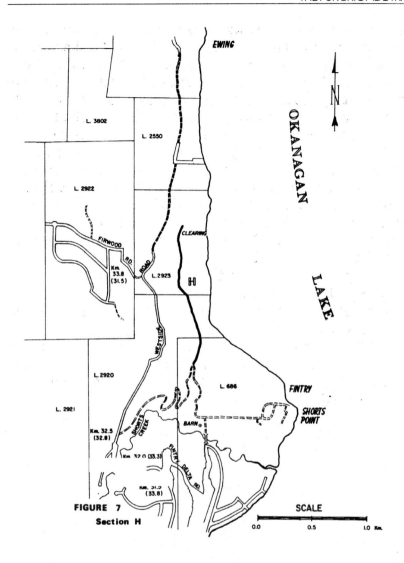

**FIGURE 7**

**Section H**

Fur Brigade locations according to Okanagan Historical Society circa 1986. *Image courtesy of Okanagan Historical Society.*

reach a rock cliff and on a granite outcrop above the trail, the pictographs are visible.

The ancient Indian art has been done in dark and light red. For those unable to locate the wall paintings, pictographs that had become loosened from the rock base in the past have been moved to the Vernon Museum.

# Chapter Two Notes

1     Barlee, N.L. *Canada West Magazine*: p 13
2     Teit, J., *The Salishan Tribes of the Western Plateaus*: Forty-fifth Annual Report of the Bureau of American Ethnology
3     Barlee, N.L. *Canada West Magazine*: p 20
4     Gellatly, D.H., *A Bit of Okanagan History*. Self-published. 1983, p 92
5     McLean, S., *The History of the O'Keefe Ranch*. UVISCO Press, Edmonton, Alberta. 1984
6     Digney, E.F., Notes for a Fintry history compiled from various sources. 1983
7     Anderson Map, 1867
8     Digney, E.F., Notes for a Fintry history compiled from various sources. 1983
9     Holt, R., A. Jahnke, and P. Tassie, *The Okanagan Brigade Trail*: Central and North Okanagan: A Field Guide to the Remaining Sections of the Trail. Vernon Branch, Okanagan Historical Society. 1986
10     Holt, R., A. Jahnke, and P. Tassie, *The Okanagan Brigade Trail*: Central and North Okanagan: A Field Guide to the Remaining Sections of the Trail: p 20 Vernon Branch, Okanagan Histori cal Society. 1986
11     ibid: p 20
12     ibid: p 22
13     ibid: p 22
14     Corner, J., *Pictographs in the Interior of British Columbia*. Wayside Press Ltd., Vernon. 1968
15     ibid

# CHAPTER THREE
## HIGH ADMIRAL OF THE OKANAGAN

When Thomas Dorling[1] Shorts spied the lush flat delta that jutted from the western shore of Lake Okanagan, it was what he probably considered an easy tour by rowboat south of the thriving area of Priest's Valley (later to be called Vernon). He was tired of wandering. At 43, he'd already been relatively unsuccessful in four careers. He'd skipped across the continent like so many other rootless men in the late 1800s, following dreams of easy wealth from the East Coast to the goldfields of California and the North Country. He wanted to settle down.

Thanks to Shorts the area we now call Fintry saw it's first glimmer of notoriety. It was Shorts who created the Okanagan's first fledgling water transport service from his small one-room cabin by the creek.

Of Dutch stock, Shorts was born on June 14, 1837 in the small village of Adolphston, Ontario, on the Bay of Quinte[2] the same year as William Lyon Mackenzie's rebellion. He spent his early childhood there before his family moved to Newburgh in Addington County, to farm.

Not much is known of his early years except perhaps that Shorts didn't see a future in farming. An inventive and imaginative character, he was the kind of man who never failed to find a way to make his way. Apparently while still in his late-teens, Shorts decided to leave Canada for the land of opportunity beckoning south of the border. His wanderings were probably idle curiosity more than anything else at first. He wasn't educated or skilled. He couldn't possibly have dreamed of becoming a captain of business in the avaricious eastern cities of America, though a "captain" of sorts is exactly what he became. Shorts was a dreamer but he wasn't a fool. With the little money he'd saved and a willingness to do just about any kind of work on offer, he started a lifelong trek that took him across the continent several times in both directions.

Shorts, it seems, relished new experiences and was not afraid to try something new if it had the chance of profit. That included selling self-threading needles from a soapbox on the streets of Philadelphia. But his youthful 'walk about' of the eastern seaboard was only temporary. The lure of California had caught his eye not long after his 20th birthday. Even though the California Gold Rush had already waned and the discoveries at Pikes Peak in Colorado were still two years away, Shorts somehow convinced himself there were plenty of chances for an enterprising young man in California. He'd been hearing the marvellous stories of gold-laden creek beds since he was ten and the first nuggets were found at Sutter's Mill. Following the 'golden glint' would have come naturally to a man like Shorts.

Shorts made his way to the Pacific and it appears easily talked himself into a job. While the back-breaking task of gold mining gave him plenty of experience that he would come to use later in his life, working for someone else didn't fit his character. Shorts outlook had been fired in the furnaces of fiercely independent United Empire Loyalist traditions. He was young, eager and stubborn. It was a character trait he would show many times, and under many different circumstances, until his death.

A brief time after arriving in California, he tossed his pick away and grabbed a push cart instead. He'd had success feeding himself with sewing needles in Philadelphia. In California he knew he could do the same and did, except instead of needles he flogged fish. When he tired of that he tried farming, fruit growing and contracting. At one point, he even managed a ranch in Mendocino County until one midnight hunt for a bothersome grizzly bear made him decide ranching was plainly too dangerous.

By the time he was 33, gold fever had infected him again. Eschewing the fish stalls for rumors of gold in British Columbia, he packed up what he needed, sold what he didn't and boarded a ship heading north. There were many men making their way towards the gold rushes at Omineca and Cassiar and he joined them happily, mining fabled streams like the Germanson, the Thibert and McDame Creek.

One story claims he collected $6,000 in gold dust in one Cassiar winter and promptly removed himself back to the U.S. Mint at Philadelphia where he had the dust specially minted into $20 gold pieces.[3] Apparently it didn't take our wanderer long to run through his poke because he soon returned to the West for more. It's reported he was one of the first to travel from the Pacific to the Peace River Plains across Frying Pan Pass and then back again by way of Stewart Lake to the Fraser River. In 1876, he found himself at the mouth of Dease Creek and in a new job as foreman for the 'Victoria' claim, one of the most noted placer mining operations in the region. While there he also got involved in the erection of the first sawmill on Dease Lake, built from machinery that had to be hauled into the wilderness by hand sleighs over 660 km (400 miles). If anything, Shorts proved his contention that men with imagination could overcome almost anything.

Gold fever had badly infected Shorts however. His early success may have been the worst thing that could have happened to him. While he accomplished many other notable goals later in life, the golden siren was always on his shoulder and whispering in his ear.

In 1881 Shorts followed her call once more with the Skagit River Rush but quickly gave up. When the Rush collapsed, he hiked from Ruby Creek to Yale and got work with the C.P.R. as a bridge builder.[4]

By 1882, Shorts' wandering found him in the Okanagan and apparently he liked what he saw. As he travelled along the old Hudson's Bay Fur Brigade Trail seeking a chunk of land on which to perch, he came across the roaring falls on Biche Creek and knew he'd found home. Most of the land along the western shore of the lake was unsettled. Access was limited to the lake and the pack-horse track. Perfect for a prospector who was used to isolation.

On July 23, 1883, perhaps following the trail to Kamloops as others had done for decades, he recorded pre-emption record Number 1165.[5] The land he recorded was later surveyed on December 30, 1888 by Vernon Civil engineer, John Coryell as Lot 686, Kamloops District (now Osoyoos District).

The British Columbia government allowed 'pre-emption' as a form of encouragement to settlement. Settlers were allowed to file claims on parcels of land up to 129 ha (320 acres) without charge. Providing they made improvements to the property to a value of $2.50 per acre within two years, they could then apply to the government for a Certificate of Improvement. With the certificate, the settler could purchase the pre-empted land for $1 per acre, paying with installments over a four year period.[6]

While those were the official requirements to gain title, the government was lenient about inspection of settlers who failed to meet the terms and often left them undisturbed in occupation of their claim.

Shorts' pre-emption of 129 ha (320 acres) at the mouth of Biche Creek took in most of the flat delta and a portion of the steep rocky hillside. Coryell's survey shows that roughly 85 ha (210 acres) of the delta was open flatland covered by gravel and sandy loam. Some pine trees of 15 cm (6 in.) to 91 cm (36 in.) diameter grew there with a belt of cottonwoods and willow brush standing along the lakefront. Coryell noted Biche Creek, dropping as it did through a steep canyon on the western boundary of the pre-emption, was possibly "an excellent waterpower" source. A.C. Anderson, mentioned in the previous chapter, also identified the waterfall on his 1867 map as a "fine mill site".[7] However, the reason it had been left unclaimed until Shorts' arrival was likely the site's inaccessibility. Good bottom land was available elsewhere and with easy access. Why bother?

The common opinion of the property didn't deter Shorts, who saw the site as having perfect access by water and isolation to boot.

Settling on the pre-emption, he called it "Fallbrook Ranch". He built himself a small cabin on the north side of the creek near the hillside and tilled a small patch of land for a garden considering what he did equal to the improvement requirements necessary for his certificate (until Coryell suggested he also needed a fence). His first and predominant crop was cabbage, a vegetable he had longed for during the long cold winters spent moiling for gold in the North.[8]

Considering the fact that what he built was only a one-room cabin and the market value of cabbages was decidedly low, its understandable why Shorts soon changed course. For the settlers sprinkled along the lake, access to supplies meant a difficult journey on horseback. Shorts had spent a brief time with the same predicament and saw opportunity calling in that hardship. He decided to have Hamill and Pringle at Spallumcheen build him a boat.

The vessel, a rowboat of 6.7 m (22 feet), was capable of carrying about 1 136 kg (2.5 tons) and he proudly christened her the Ruth Shorts in honour of his mother. With entrepreneurial zeal, he bought supplies in Spallumcheen and then freighted them to Penticton and the ready market waiting there, particularly among the Indians on the reservation.

While capable of hoisting a small sail, "the principal propelling power was a white-ash breeze which had its Aeolian abode in the stout muscles of Shorts' back and arms."[9]

"For three years in fair weather and in foul, he ran this boat and at last became so accustomed to the oars that he could row from morning until night without weariness."[10]

Shorts' success immediately attracted the attention of established Penticton merchants, particularly Thomas Ellis.[11] Ellis, a cattle rancher, had built a lucrative business hauling goods over the mountains to Penticton from Hope using pack trains.[12] As one of the wealthiest, and therefore most powerful residents in the area, Ellis evidently didn't take kindly to the new form of competition. In quick order Shorts was convinced his future lay in freighting rather than merchandising and the Okanagan's first freight service via the lake was born.

"Captain" Shorts, as he quickly became known, was soon to be found hauling not only cargo but also the occasional passenger on the nine-day, 125 km (75 mile) journey down Okanagan Lake.[13] He enjoyed his new occupation and the salty caricature he could play as a mariner.

Shorts was "very much what we should describe as a 'live wire'. He was a very assertive little man, with a face almost buried in a snuffy beard of no particular color, which bore the visual evidence of the fact that he chewed tobacco; he really looked snuffy all over. He always wore a very faded bowler hat, cocked down over one eye in a sporty way — I doubt if anyone had ever seen him without it. He had an amazing flow of language with which he would describe his many adventures or induce you to help finance his hopeful business enterprises, for he was so chock-full of optimism that he was very persuasive."[14]

The comic reports of Shorts' rowing passengers down the lake are many. He did it in a style uniquely his own. For example, like most other matters concerning Shorts, schedules were variable. If asked how long the trip would take, his patented reply always was "I haven't the faintest idea, but rest assured we'll fetch up there sometime!"[15] The trips were never speedy and rarely dull. He would row during the day and as night began to fall, pull into any handy beach available and set up a camp under a tree. Any passengers along for the ride would share the tree with Shorts, unless of course they felt the need to escape his stories, in which case they might find a tree of their own.

The trips were not known for the frills of comfort that other captains might throw in for paying passengers, as one account describes.

"The captain and a passenger were once marooned on the wrong side of the lake — that is, on the side on which there was no trail, for a whole week of stormy weather. Luckily this did not happen when he was carrying a lady as his only passenger — her experience was alarming enough as it was — for her. That trip fortunately took only three days; they camped overnight on the shore; she sleeping under one tree and the captain under another. She was an English girl of gentle birth, on her way to the family of a rancher where she was to act as governess — one would expect her to be filled with misgivings; for the captain's appearance was not such as to inspire confidence, but as she told me about it some time afterwards, her sense of humour had evidently made her enjoy the somewhat unconventional experience; at any rate, as she said, it was something

41

to write home about."[16]

Captain Shorts operated in this unique way for three years and is a reported to have earned himself $6,000 in the process. But, the work was hard by any standard of measure. In 1885 a visiting Victoria Indian agent, showed Shorts a different way, a way of modern progress. Dr. I. W. Powell, having no doubt experienced the long and somewhat boring trip in Short's rowboat, advised the entrepreneurial captain that modern marine technology had arrived and he wondered why the Captain hadn't taken advantage.[17] Powell described a coal-oil burning engine that was being advertised in magazines of the day as a mechanical way to easily propel skiffs without the back-bending labor that Shorts was exhibiting on the Ruth Shorts.[18] "With an engine such as that," Powell is likely to have counselled, "the trips will be shorter and you can make more of them."

Shorts had already been considering a move up in vessel class for reasons of what he likely suspected would be unfair competition. On July 16, 1861 in a dispatch to the Home Government, Governor Douglas had suggested opening up the country to settlement by placing steamboats on Shuswap Lake and Okanagan Lake. A wagon road from Ashcroft to Savana's Ferry had been completed and a steamboat already placed on Shuswap Lake.[19] With the wagon road from Okanagan Lake to Spallumcheen Prairie in place, could it be long before another government boat would be plying his private waters?

With information about the coal-oil powered engine and proof in the lucrative potential in freighting goods and passengers, Captain Shorts sought an investor. He convinced Thomas Greenhow, one of the first drovers to push cattle along the Hudson's Bay Fur Brigade Trail and now a well-off rancher, to part with some cash and invest it in his steam boating venture. With Greenhow's financial assistance, Shorts ordered one of the two-horsepower automatic coal-burning engines manufactured in Rochester, New York. At the same time he commissioned boat-builders at Lansdowne, to construct a new vessel so he would have a lake-worthy boat to use it.

The engine may have been the leading edge of technology at the time, but is was certainly not a miracle of miniaturization. According to newspaper reports "it was about the size of a medium stove and weighed 700 lbs."[20] The hull built at Lansdowne was hauled to the Okanagan by wagon,[21] the engine eventually installed and the 45 cm (18-inch prop) attached.

On April 21, 1886, the "Mary Victoria Greenhow" was launched. The vessel, named after the only daughter of Thomas and Elizabeth Greenhow, was 9.75 m (32 ft) long with a 1.5 m (5 ft) beam. The launch party was transported to Fallbrook Ranch where Shorts happily entertained them with predictions of huge success to come.

Within a few days, Shorts was proudly standing at the helm and ready to take his first trip south. The Captain undoubtedly considered the Mary V. Greenhow a huge step up in class, so much so it's reported that he discarded his Bowler and doffed a sea-captain's cap in honour of the occasion. On that first run, the Mary V. Greenhow not only carried her registered limit of five tons in freight and five passengers, but Shorts had magnanimously agreed to also tow another boat to Penticton.[22] The small two-horse engine may have been ideal for skinny punts, but what Shorts was demanding of it didn't make sense. It averaged only five knots per hour when loaded and eight knots when empty and the coal-oil engine "took a whole match factory to set it working."[23]

The Captain fully expected the barrel of coal-oil aboard would be ample to the task of the run to Penticton and back but he soon learned otherwise. Chugging into Penticton for the first time with less fuel than he needed to get home however, still warranted suitable welcome. A happy crowd of miners and pack train attendants awaited the Mary V. Greenhow and Shorts was formally recognized with an ebullient 21-shotgun salute.

The return trip up the lake was another matter. Shorts found himself leap frogging from settler's cabin to cabin all along the way. The excited residents would welcome the steamer and Shorts would promptly talk them out of their coal-oil. By the time he returned to the dock and his waiting partner in Vernon, Shorts' engine was not the only thing steaming.

"Tom Greenhow, we're a busted institution, that's what. We are ruined; one more trip like that and we are a financial wreck!"[24] It was well into the night before Shorts finished the story, with reports that both he and Greenhow bent over roaring with laughter wondering about the lantern-less nature of the lake that night.

The Mary V Greenhow continued to ply the lake four months longer, a regular cause of grief to its captain.

"The last trip she made seems to have been a chapter of mishaps for when leaving the Head of the Lake the wind was blowing strong from the South and among other things in the cargo was a pig in a crate for Shorts' ranch. They were in pretty much of a quandary what to do with the pig as there was no one on the ranch and if they turned it loose it would eat up the garden that had been planted or if left in the crate it would starve to death before the boat returned. So Bill Clark (one of Shorts' crew) said he would get off and look after the pig as he would rather be along with the pig than on the boat on such a day."[25]

On the return journey, as had become a reluctant expectation, the boat was running low on fuel. Shorts decided to stop at Okanagan Mission to spend the night at Lequime's where he could obtain more fuel. During the night however, the Mary V. Greenhow, whose planks were soaked with coal-oil, caught fire and burned to the waterline along with freight belonging to Lequime and Tom Ellis.[26]

"Next morning the captain viewed the remains of his ill-fated craft and thus soliloquized "well I'm through with you now, anyhow; and blame my eyes if it isn't a darn good job.""[27]

Shorts nevertheless salvaged equipment from the burnt hulk and moved it to Okanagan Landing. Within a few weeks he had acquired a sailboat of three tons capacity from Brewer and Tronson and by September 20 had installed the equipment and was once again on the lake.[28]

In the months that followed, Shorts and Greenhow tried to convert the coal-oil engine to a wood-burner but were unsuccessful. They finally conceded the coal-oil contraption had been a mistake and ordered a new boiler. It arrived in July 1887 and Shorts with the help of a ship's carpenter named John Hamilton, built a 9 m (30ft) clinker boat with an 2.4 m (8 ft) beam to house it. The boiler was installed and the new vessel was ready to be launched on September 22, 1887, christened the Jubilee in honour of Queen Victoria's Golden Jubilee. Shorts, rather patriotically, also renamed the creek on his property Jubilee Creek at the same time.

With an estimated 20 men from Priest's Valley to help, the launch was undertaken.

"...and exactly at the hour of 3.30 the launch of the 'Jubilee' was successfully made amid cheers from the crowd. The union Jack was immediately unfurled; and, as is usual in all launches, a bottle of wine was broken over the bow of the craft...a short spurt down the lake proved the excellent sea-going qualities and swiftness of the boat. The party returned to the village immediately afterwards, highly pleased with success of the day. The worthy captain's health was proposed and drank with great enthusiasm."[29]

A fair vessel in comparative standards, the Jubilee plied the lake without incident until 1889. That year, a gold strike had been made in the Similkameen on Granite Creek. Shorts knew perfectly what the gold-seeking miners needed in the way of supplies. With two merchants from Lansdowne (Wood and Rabbitt) Shorts had a warehouse built on the beach at Summerland to help facilitate the shipment of goods from there to the Similkameen by pack train. He kept the Jubilee busy freighting supplies from Okanagan Landing to Storehouse Point (now Crescent Beach) and even built a barge he could tow behind the Jubilee for overflow freight.

Business was so good at the time, it prompted two other men, Porteous and Gillies, to resurrect a steamboat that had sunk in Spallumcheen and press the repaired vessel into service on Okanagan Lake in competition with Shorts on July 19, 1888. They called it the Okanagan.

The captain's new steamboat schedule was no more reliable than any other boat he steered down the lake.

Hester E. White (nee Haynes) recalled a trip on the Jubilee. Taken beginning on October 15, 1888 at the age of 11, with her mother, two other women and five siblings, she remembered that "because we had enjoyed previous trips on the Fraser River boats between Hope and New Westminster it was a disappointment to think we must travel the seventy miles (112 km) to the Head of the Lake in this miserable little craft (Jubilee).

"Captain Shorts in overalls and jacket, a peaked cap over one eye, was smoking a very strong corncob pipe — held to one side of his mouth. All this and his tobacco-stained beard made him a typical 'Pop-eye, the sailor-man'.

"Harry Tilliard and a 'ty-hee' (boss) Chinaman were passengers and, together with Captain Shorts and (Clement) Vachie (the roustabout), occupied the stern of the boat. With the engine in the centre, little space was left to accommodate Mother, Connie, Matilda and six children in the bow, on each side of which was a narrow seat. Wood was piled near the very small engine. A canvas was spread over the top of the boat to shelter us.

"The kitchen-box containing a cooked ham, some cold chickens, which had their heads shot off the day before, part of a sack of potatoes and, no doubt, bread, butter, etc. was put on board. That was the day's rations, for we expected to be but one day on the boat.

"With a toot of the whistle, much noise and much smell as the (Jubilee) was backing out into the blue sparkling waters of the lake, Tom Ellis shouted, 'Will you make head of the lake tonight, Captain?' and the answer was 'Sure thing!' He was much too optimistic for we had a head wind, and with a heavy load and a bulky scow in tow, we had to tie up that evening at what is now Crescent Beach. Camp was made and we settled down for the night.

"We were off early next morning and were thankful to arrive safely that night at the Lambly Ranch beach. Only by the Grace of God had we survived a heavy squall round Squally Point, when waves washed over the boat and the engine stopped. The Captain, not very sea-worthy at that moment, was pushed aside by Tilliard, who had discovered that the boiler was nearly dry. It was leaking badly and it was told how oatmeal had

45

been thrown in to plug the leak.

"We had great difficulty landing in the storm, but fires were soon lighted to warm us and dry out our clothes and bedding. Clement Vachie disappeared into the woods and everyone rejoiced when he came back with a year-old buck over his shoulder. For our kitchen-box now contained only potatoes...

"Next morning the Okanagan passed us again for the third or fourth time...

"That night we beached at the Mission on the east side of the lake. We were greatly surprised and pleased to have Father Pandosy and one of his lay-brothers visit our camp to bring Mother fruit, vegetables, and other gifts...

"The fourth day was our last in the miserable little boat when we arrived at the head of the lake."[30]

Sometimes the irregular schedule that Shorts kept was not his fault at all. Harry Colbeck, an engine operator trained in Britain who had arrived in Okanagan in 1889 seeking work, recalls his first meeting with the memorable Captain Shorts.

"I was in the Victoria Hotel when a man came in with a full red beard, an old straw hat on. They called him Captain Shorts. He was very angry. He said 'My Engineer is drunk and I can't get out and I have a man with a big outfit going to Grand Prairie. If I could find another man, I would put that fellow ashore quick, but what few men I know are out on thrashing machines."[31]

Colbeck told Shorts of his training and he was immediately taken on the vessel as a trial run to test his experience. He and Shorts were the only crew. They had one passenger, the owner of a grain binder that was loaded as freight along with several barrels of whiskey. Colbeck recalled the owner came aboard with a sheaf of wheat under one arm and as soon as the boat got underway he bored a hole in one of the barrels and began sucking whiskey with a wheat straw.

On that trip there was no need to stop at Short's property to take on wood for the boiler. They arrived on schedule with the binder owner listing a little to starboard.

Having enough wood on board however, wasn't always the case. Often, Shorts would make for Jubilee Creek if he was running short of fuel.

He "landed all hands including the passengers, and insisted that everyone cut enough wood for the trip...

"The passengers, in spite of their efforts with axe and bucksaw, still paid their full fare! In the event their performance wasn't up to the captain's liking they heard about it in no uncertain terms."

The fall of 1889 was fateful for Shorts and for his property. That October while he was on a trip to get his mail, the proprietor of the Victoria Hotel hailed Shorts in the street.

"There are two Englishmen at the hotel who want to shoot big horn sheep," he told Shorts. "I told them to talk to you."

Because the delta that Shorts called home provided the best access to big sheep country in the Okanagan, Shorts agreed to collect up the hunters, their guns, their baggage, guide and cook and ferry them in the Jubilee to Fallbrook Ranch. For two weeks the cook and the guide showed the visitors the way to the big horn while Shorts rushed supplies to the waiting miners.

When he returned to pick them up, the two men were effusive in their compliments about the area and described how they wanted to build a shooting lodge right there where they were standing. They asked Shorts who the lucky owner of the delta might be and he proudly tugged his cap. When they asked how much he would ask for the property Shorts grinned and gave the ridiculously expensive price of $4,000.

Shorts hardly expected the men to respond. The Captain had tried to sell the property for years and instead of rising, his price got cheaper by the year.

Shorts had offered the land for a song to Tom Butters in May 1892: "I saw a man ploughing the soil which looked rich and black. I talked to him of the soil and crops grown, then talked of his horses and my wanting one. He told me Captain Shorts had a good cayuse for sale so I held the plow until we reached the other end and then walked down the railroad to Okanagan Landing and found Shorts. We bargained for the horse. I was to pay $30 if it suited. He got a man to ride up the range side and bring it in. I gave him two dollars for doing this for it took him about half an hour. I went in and had dinner with Shorts and his wife, a very intelligent woman. We talked of the country and Cap Shorts wanted to sell me a pre-emption on a point down the lake. He said a house on the place was worth $600 and he would sell everything for $600, but I did not fancy having to row a boat to get there and there was no other way to get out. After dinner they lent me a saddle and I rode back to Vernon."[32]

Only a few weeks earlier, Shorts had confessed to hating the property and tried to interest Harry Colbeck, his apprentice engineer on the Jubilee in buying it. All he was able to grow there were cabbages, he claimed, and at the night the hoot owls scared him out of his wits. Shorts had offered to sell the property to Colbeck for $75 but Colbeck declined, thinking the price too high.

47

S.S. Sicamous, circa 1920s. *Photo courtesy of O'Keefe Historic Ranch archive.*

With a secret grin, the Captain directed the cook and guide in loading the visitors' belongings while the two foreign men conversed in hushed tones.

The price seemed reasonable, they finally said. "We will place the money in escrow in the Bank of Montreal in Victoria and when you place the title in the Bank, you get the money."

This windfall, unexpected as it was, couldn't have come at a better time for our hapless Captain Shorts. That winter in a sudden cold snap, the Jubilee was frozen in the ice at Okanagan Landing and later sunk. Shorts salvaged the machinery in the spring and installed it on a large, unwieldy barge he grandly named the City of Vernon. The Jubilee had "survived her usefulness"[33] in Shorts opinion which might have been why he didn't care too much that she would await winter in relatively shallow water.

He hurriedly completed the necessary requirements to get title on the pre-empted property. On January 18, 1890, after paying $320, Shorts was given a Crown Grant of title to the 320 acres of Lot 686, Kamloops District (now Osoyoos District). He promptly conveyed title on February 3 to the Hon. John Walter Edward Scott-Douglas-Montague and to Richard Granville Hare Viscount Ennismore. Scott-Douglas-Montague was son and heir to Lord Henry John Scott-Douglas-Montague, baron Montague of Beaulieu. Hare was son of William Hare, the 3rd Earl of Listowel.

Shorts removed the engine and other components he could from the Jubilee that winter and mounted them to his barge. This was, however, only temporary. Upon viewing the vessel most prospective customers were less than impressed. One described the City of Vernon as "a little tub of doubtful safety with a very obvious homemade look about her"[34]

Once the Captain had received his payment for Fallbrook Ranch, he promptly went to Vancouver where he arranged for yet another vessel, and ordered a new engine and boiler from manufacturers in Toronto. In April 1890, with Tom Ellis as his partner in the venture, Shorts laid the keel for a new steamer at Okanagan Landing.

By August the Penticton, was lake-worthy. Mistakenly identified as the Pentoctin by a French-Canadian workman hired to paint her name on the hull (a name she carried for some time), she was a 21.3 m (70 ft). long behemoth. With 4.8 m (16 ft) of beam, twin screws and 50 tonne (50 ton) gross weight, she was launched in September 1890 with as much pomp as the less remarkable M.V. Greenhow had received years before her.

While she may have been licensed to carry 25 passengers, the Penticton sported only a tiny cabin for their comfort, furnished with a few stools and one Morris chair.

Shorts may have had a new boat, but his old habits of independence continued. The schedule for the Penticton was haphazard at best until July 30 of the following year[35] when he finally attempted to run a weekly schedule but even that was unreliable. If Shorts took a dislike to anyone in Kelowna, he was just a liable to cruise on past Kelowna as he was to drop off the freight or passengers he'd been paid to deliver[36]. Even the likes of the venerable Lord Aberdeen couldn't get Shorts and his crew to forego an all-night dance at the 1891 Vernon Fall Fair and make the passage when Shorts had his mind on other things. Aberdeen, it is claimed, was forced to beg a ride to Kelowna with Leo Lequime in the storekeeper's steam-launch,[37] explaining sadly that the reason was the notorious Captain. Lequime evidently understood.

In spite of his habits and the fact the Penticton wasn't proving profitable as an enterprise because of them, it didn't stop Shorts many friends and customers from recognizing him as a valley celebrity. He was still immensely popular, so popular in fact, a group of his friends hosted a special affair at the Kalamalka Hotel in Vernon to offer the Captain a special title, that of 'High Admiral of the Okanagan'[38]

In a brief recount of Shorts career a few years later, the Vernon News reported:

"What Balboa was to the Pacific so in a measure was Capt. Shorts to the Okanagan, but he differed from the early navigators in that his early voyages were not voyages of discovery. 'We were the first that ever burst, Into that silent sea' has been the proud boast of many a proud navigator who for the nonce was less a public benefactor than was Capt. Shorts with his load of bacon and flour from the lone prospector or the weary rancher, down the lake."[39]

In 1892, at the age of 55 and two years after the Penticton was launched, Shorts sold the boat to Leon Lequime and his brother for $5,000.[40] Shorts no doubt knew his time as the valley's freight-meister were numbered because if it wasn't government talking about steamboating on Okanagan Lake, it was the deep-pocketed C.P.R. The Canadian Pacific Railway had decided there was a future of profit to be made and they'd begun to build a sternwheeler for that purpose at Okanagan Landing. Shorts probably decided it was time, once again, to move on.

The C.P.R. Aberdeen was completed and launched into service in May 1893, forcing the Penticton into use by the Kelowna Sawmill Co. for towing log booms.

Freedom from his freighting business gave Shorts time to dream up new schemes. Shorts had considered starting a business supplying trout out of Okanagan Lake and he tried to revive an older scheme of his to build a canal to connect the Thompson River system with the Okanagan[41]. He considered raising hay and hogs from his ranch in the White Valley near Vernon as well, even boasting his expectations that "there's millions in it"[42] but eventually returned to his first career love: mining. Purchasing a claim from Mitchell Jarvice on Harris Creek[43] he began to mine with Charles Brewer, but that only lasted until the Fall. In September he sold his half-interest to Tom Ellis who had discovered a coal lode near Okanagan Lake.[44]

For a while, it appears Shorts did not do much of anything but in 1895, mustering his trademarked optimism, Shorts told his friends he'd decided that the real opportunity now lay back in the North. News of the Klondike gold discovery was leaking out to the South and Shorts knew it was more than rumor. Not everyone agreed. As the Vernon News commented on his departure: "When the captain believes anything, he believes it pretty throughly."

By 1897, Shorts had made his way to Juneau, Alaska with thousands of other belated seekers. He saw quickly he was too late there as he had been in California, but after a muscle-torturing climb up the White Pass, he also saw an opportunity. Rather than mining, Shorts attempted to garner support amongst the visionaries in Alaska to build a tramway for 11 km (7 miles) up the canyon to the rapids. Sadly, because of his age perhaps or the fact he had none of his own money to risk on the venture, his vision didn't see reality. A year later though, someone else did just that.

Shorts stayed in the Yukon and Alaska for some time, finally returning to the South to settle in Hope, B.C. with dreams of starting a lumber mill. By 1912 however, his age was working against him. At 75 years-old he finally gave up and moved into a small cabin where he lived, poor and alone until his death on February 9, 1921, aged 83.

# Chapter Three Notes

1  Vital Statistics Division, in a reply to the Provincial Archives, reported their records show his middle name as Dorling, not Dolman as otherwise reported

2  Vernon News, March 1892, p 1

3  ibid, March 17, 1892, p 5

4  Gray, A.W., *Pioneer Navigator of the Okanagan Passes*, Okanagan Historical Society. Thirty-fifth Report: 1971, p 151; Vancouver Province, February 19, 1921

5  Weeks, Captain J.B., *Steamboating on Okanagan Lake*. The Sixth Report of the Okanagan Historical Society: 1935, p 225

6  Cail, R.E., *Land, Man and the Law: The Disposal of Crown Lands in British Columbia, 1871-1913*, Vancouver: University of British Columbia Press, 1974, pp 23, 28, 33, 253

7  Harvey, A.G., *Okanagan Place Names: Their Origin and Meaning*. The Twelfth Report of the Okanagan Historical Society: 1948, p 219

8  Vernon News, November 17, 1838. p 4

9  ibid, June 15, 1893, p 1

10  ibid

11  ibid, March 17, 1892, p 5

12  Weeks, Captain J.B., *The History of Steamboats on Okanagan Lake*, undated msss, Kelowna Museum Archives

13  Vernon News, June 15, 1893, p 1

14  Holliday, C.W., *The Valley of Youth*, Caldwell, Idaho: Caxton Printers:1948, pp 208-209

15  Weeks, Captain J.B., *The History of Steamboats on Okanagan Lake*, undated mss, Kelowna Museum Archives, p 224

16  Holliday, C.W., *The Valley of Youth*, Caldwell, Idaho:Caxton Printers:1948, pp 208-209

17  Norris, L., *The First Steamboat on Okanagan Lake*. The Sixth Report of the Okanagan Historical Society: 1935, p 260

18  Gosselin, J., *The Real Estate Review*: September 10, 1987, p 4

19  ibid

20  Inland Sentinel: February 25, 1886

21  Young, B.F., *Early Days in British Columbia*. The Sixth Report of the Okanagan Historical Society: 1935, p 256

22  Gosselin, J., *The Real Estate Review*: September 10, 1987, p 4

23  Vernon News: March 17, 1892, p 5

24   Gosselin, J., *The Real Estate Review*: September 10, 1987, p 4
25   Weeks, Captain J.B., *The History of Steamboats on Okanagan Lake*, undated msss, Kelowna Museum Archives, pp 2-3
26   Vernon News: March 17, 1892, p 5
27   ibid: June 15, 1893, p 1
28   Inland Sentinel: September 30, 1886, p 3
29   ibid: September 24, 1887, p 2
30   White, H.E., *On Okanagan Lake in 1888: Four Days in Captain Shorts' Boat*. The Eighteenth     Report of the Okanagan Historical Society: 1954, pp 43-45
31   Letter written to William McCulloch by Harry Colbeck, December 12, 1940, copy in Kamloops Museum Archives
32   Butters, T.H., The Fourteenth Report of the Okanagan Historical Society: 1950, p 78
33   Vernon News: July 15, 1883, p 1
34   Holliday, C.W., *The Valley of Youth*, Caldwell, Idaho:Caxton Printers:1948, pp 208
35   Vernon News: July 30, 1891, p 7
36   Interview of Gordon Haug by Imbert Orchard, November 7, 1965.  Tape in Provincial Archives of British Columbia, Victoria, accession 1125
37   Pentland, M., *Salute by an Oldtimer*. The Eighteenth Report of the Okanagan Historical Soci    ety: 1954, p 8
38   Vernon News: November 19, 1891, p 5
39   ibid: June 15, 1893, p 1
40   ibid: March 17, 1892, p 5
41   Inland Sentinel: March 19, 1887, p 3
42   Morkill, G.H., *The Shuswap and Okanagan Railway Company*. The Third Report of the Okanagan Historical Society: 1929, pp 10-12
43   Vernon News: October 6, 1892, p 7
44   ibid: July 20, 1893, p 5

# CHAPTER FOUR
## THE PIECES THAT MADE FINTRY

The two young men who bought 'Shorts' Point' were sporting dilettantes. Hare was a member of the Eton 'Shooting Eight'[1] Both were born to wealth and more familiar in their mid-20's with exotic hunting safaris than the demands of an occupation.

At the time of the purchase, Richard Granville Hare was 24 and as son of the 3rd Earl of Listowel, carried the title of Viscount Ennismore. Educated at Eton and Oxford, his visit to Canada with John Walter Edward Douglas-Scott-Montagu was little more than a wealthy man's 'walk about'. They came for trophies and little more. Considered so unimportant in fact, the visit and purchase is not even recorded in an otherwise detailed family history written by the current Earl of Listowel. One can assume therefore that the purchase was a whimsy by the two men and quickly forgotten in the turmoil of more exciting affairs that immediately followed their visit.

On his return to Great Britain, Hare spent his time at leisure, salmon fishing in the River Blackwater at Convamore and shooting woodcock in the surrounding woodlands, his property in Canada seemingly forgotten. While in Ireland during the years that followed his return he became Master of the Duhallow Hunt, and because of that status he was encouraged to defend Britain's honor in the Anglo-Boer War of 1899-1902.

Hare joined the 13th Battalion of Imperial Yeomanry Cavalry to serve as a second Lieutenant in the 1st Life Guards under the command of British regular, Lieutenant Colonel Basil Spragge. "To British eyes, this mounted Battalion was the social and political show-piece of the new Volunteer Army; a company of Irish M.F.H.'s known as the Irish Hunt

Contingent, including the Earl of Longford and Viscount Ennismore; two companies of Ulster Protestant Unionists, including the Earl of Leitrim, a whiskey Baronet (Sir John Power) and the future Lord Craigavon; and a company of English and Irish men-about-town raised by Lord Donoughmore, who had insisted on paying their own passage to South Africa."[2]

On May 31, 1890, only a few weeks after his arrival in Africa, Hare's unit faced Piet de Wet's troops in a battle that resulted in their surrender after 80 of the gentlemen troopers were killed or wounded. Much to the humorous delight in nationalist circles back in Ireland, 530 of Spragge's Irish Yeomanry served the remainder of the hostilities in a prisoner of war camp. In spite of his short career, Hare was nonetheless

Piet de Wet poses for a victory photo.

awarded the Queen's Medal with three clasps upon his return to England.

At the age of 48, Hare rejoined his old regiment, the Royal Munster Fusiliers on the outbreak of the First World War in 1914. Because of his age he wasn't considered fit for regular service and instead became a Provost Marshall in the Mediterranean and later in Cairo. After the war he retired with the rank of Major, living out his life gardening and hunting. With the death of his father in 1924, Hare succeeded to the peerage to become the 4th Earl of Listowel and died eight years later from pneumonia contracted after a day's shooting in the rain with a neighbour, Sir Trehawke Kekewich.

Hare's partner in the purchase succeeded in making a larger mark.

As the first son and heir to Lord Henry John Douglas-Scott-Montagu, first Baron Montagu of Beaulieu, John Walter Edward also loved to hunt almost as much as he loved politics and driving automobiles.

Upon his return from Canada, he ran for the Conservative Seat in New Forest in 1892 and served as an MP[3] until his father's death in 1905, at which time he succeeded to the peerage as the second Baron Montagu of Beaulieu.[4]

His greatest claims to fame centered around the automobile. As a pioneer enthusiast of the motorcar, in 1900 he gave King Edward VII his first ride two years before the King's coronation. He was an avid collector (many of the automobiles he owned are now on display at his son's National Motor Museum at Beaulieu, Hants) but he's most famous for having failed in a battle to see the speed limit removed from Britain's roads and creating the need for license plates.

In 1903 the speed limit in Britain was 12.5 mph and the fine for exceeding it was 10 pounds. That made it an offence equivalent in law to "harbouring thieves knowingly" or "selling poisoned grain".

Among the 120-odd "motoring MPs" at the time, he wanted the speed limit abolished completely and replaced with the offence of "furious driving" outlined in a 1835 Act that was originally intended to control dangerous horsemen. His Bill, based on suggestion from the Legislative Committee of the Automobile Club, was aimed at giving drivers "greater freedom of speed" in exchange for the introduction of number plates on the motor cars.

After two attempts at getting second reading for his Bill failed, the Government introduced its own - virtually identical - Motor-Cars Bill in the House of Lords. It raised the speed limit to 20 mph and forced motorists to show that they were responsible citizens, register their motor cars, display number plates and take out driving licences.

While the two young men found the mountains near Shorts' Point idyllic for hunting, they never returned to Canada to make use of their ownership. Neither did they send money or workmen to build their shooting lodge.

As time passed the property became derelict with various casual visitors calling it home. In 1892, the Vernon News noted "this beautiful piece of property was running wild"[5] and a popular spot for picnics.

"Shorts' ranch or Fall creek is the best known point (for excursions on Okanagan Lake),perhaps, as much on account of the magnificent waterfall and canyon as for its proximity to Goat Mountain, where big game can always be found by the venturesome."[6]

The vacant property acted as a magnet to prospectors who wandered up the creek from the falls in search of gold, to squatters just spending a season and drifters hiding from the law.

An account paints a descriptive picture of the types of men who found their way to peace along Shorts' Creek.

One winter afternoon, Billy Holliday[7] was travelling down the westside of the Okanagan Lake when he encountered a likeable fellow named Jacob Laur who was known as 'Montana Jake'. With night soon to fall, Jake invited Billy to visit with him and his partner "Fatty Brown" in their cabin, a long climb up a steep trail from the falls.

"It was secluded, all right, hidden among the trees in a little hollow by a creek — I don't think any creditors or whatever they were would be likely to bother them there. At one end of the cabin was a rough lean-to where Jake told me to put my horse...and going to the cabin door was introduced to Fatty, and realized how he had come by his name; for he was the exact opposite of Jake, who was lean and wiry. Fatty's beard was also red, but it spread out wide like a fan; his face was fat and coarse and he had an enormous stomach; in fact, whereas Jake was rather a comical figure and everyone liked him, Fatty had rather a truculent appearance and there was a shifty look in his eyes. I imagine his covering of fat protected him from the cold, for his upper parts were clad only in a red flannel undershirt."

After a meal of beans, flapjacks and syrup washed down with strong tea the men relaxed.

"And after supper we smoked and yarned, and they told me they were running a horse ranch up here, although I had seen no evidence of horses — there was not even a corral. But I suppose they felt they had to give some reason for living here.

"The little sheet-iron stove was kept well-stoked — they evidently liked warmth; soon the fog in the cabin was so thick you could have re-moved it with a shovel, and uneasy thoughts assailed me, where was I going to sleep: The cabin was very small, with an earth floor; the table and stove, a few blocks of wood, and a wide box of a bed in one corner just filled it. I soon found out. 'Well,' said Jake — his head had been nodding sleepily for some time; 'I guess it's about time we hit the hay; Billy's a little feller an' won't take much room, so he'd better sleep in the middle.' Heaven forbid, thought I — my misgivings had not been without reason. But so it had to be, although by exercising a little tact I did manage to get the outside place on the bed. I thought longingly of the fresh air outside, where I could have rolled up comfortably in my blankets in the pile of hay; and mildly suggested that rather than put them to incon-venience I would do this, but 'Hell no; there's lots of room here, Billy'; so being too polite to press the point I accepted my doom. Fatty, like an enormous snoring pig occupied the middle of the bed, while I squeezed myself as close to the outside edge as I could, the stove about two feet from my head and Fatty's posterior, about as hot as another stove, stick-ing into my back. In my time I have slept in many uncomfortable places but this one had them all beaten."

There were other settlers in the area though, of a more publicly acceptable standard.

E.J. Wilson had a ranch five miles up Shorts' Creek and had constructed a cabin even further into the mountains to act as accommodation for hunting parties for whom he would guide on occasion.[8] Wilson, like so many other settlers in the area at that time, was also avidly prospecting and in 1896 registered several claims in partnership with J. Tingley including the 'Early Riser', 'Big Horn' and 'Surprise' claims.[9] Wilson was industrious and opportunistic, apparently tackling many varied schemes where cash could be had. In 1896, he along with Tingley and J.B. Bruce build a wharf on Bruce's property near Shorts' Point that was capable of accommodating the C.P.R. steamer Aberdeen. The dock was built so the men could fulfill a contract to supply 350 cords of firewood to the steamer that winter[10] but the dock had much more historic purpose for the Okanagan that would be realized later.

Sometime after 1897 and before 1905, Wilson vacated his property in the mountains above Shorts' Point and it was taken over by a British immigrant named Tom Hamilton.

Not too far up Short's Creek, an American Civil War veteran had also settled. E. Hercules Love had served under General Ulysses S. Grant and following the war, worked as a cattle drover. It is suspected that he first saw the Okanagan during one of the cattle drives from Washington to the Cariboo gold fields between 1858 and 1860. During the cattle drive it was rumoured that Love recognized loose pieces of gold ore in Shorts' Creek and returned after reaching the Cariboo to seek the mother lode.

A claim he called 'Home Stake' was staked in 1903. It was 139 sq. m (1,500 sq ft) on the south bank of Shorts' Creek on the slope of a mountain that was then called Zion Mountain. Love worked the claim for the next five years and by 1908 had driven a tunnel that started 3 m (10 ft) above the level of the creek, ran south for 27 m (90 ft) and then turned east for 22.8 , (75 ft). At a depth of about 26 m (85 ft) he found a 38 cm (15 in) vein of low-grade ore that assayed at only $2 to $5 per ton.

"Although nothing worthwhile has yet been struck, the indications of the rock through which Mr. Love has driven his 165-foot tunnel has inspired him with unbounded faith in the ground he is prospecting."[11] Love had also staked a placer claim for the creek bed outside his mine where he hand-dug a shaft 40-feet before finally being driven out by seeping water. Love calculated that he would need a 1300-ft drainage tunnel to allow him to gain access to the bedrock in the area and he hand-dug 150-feet before quitting in disgust.

But Love was an optimist. A neighbour recalls: "He was a small wiry old man with a long white beard and as I remember him he seemed a bundle of energy, probably in his late 70s. With unflagging optimism he was always on the verge of striking the 'pay lode' though he was already

61 m (200 ft) or more into the mountain. How he handled his rock drill and sledge hammer alone I'll never know. He would spend a large part of his American Army pension on dynamite and coal for his small forge and lived in a tiny log dugout where he could sit on his bunk and reach everything else in the cabin. About once a week he hiked down the Creek trail

Tom Hamilton's first ranch house located in meadows several kilometers above Shorts' Creek delta, circa 1897. *Photograph courtesy of the O'Keefe Historical Ranch Archives.*

to Tom's ranch some 3 miles (4.8 km) to pick up his mail and supplies and back-packed it to his cabin. Tom occasionally helped with a pack horse to take dynamite and coal. With people he knew he loved to yarn about early days on the plains, but with strangers he became shy and reticent, punctuating his brief remarks with profanity."[12] Love finally gave up on his hunt in 1915 and returned to the U.S. where he lived the rest of his life with an elderly sister in Kittitas County.

As well as prospectors, Shorts' Point delta attracted a man who wanted to grow more than cabbages as Captain Shorts had done. David Erskine Gellatly leased the property from its' distant owners during the Spring of 1895.[13]

Gellatly and his wife Eliza emigrated to Canada in 1883, originally planning to settle in the northern bushland of Ontario. They spent a decade there, having nearly half as many children as they did crops[14] before David heard the call of the West. In 1893 they made the journey to Vernon where Gellatly found work as a carpenter for two years. But the urge to

Hercule Love, circa 1908. A Civil War veteran, Love hand-drilled long tunnels through the bedrock of Goat Mountain in search of an illusive vein of gold he belived would launch another gold rush.
*Photograph courtesy of B.C. Properties Ltd.*

see things grow pulled at him. After taking several hunting trips up Shorts' Creek (he bagged at least eight bighorn rams, including two with horns measuring more than 35.5 cm (14 in) at the base[15]), in the Fall of 1894 Gellatly came to realize the potential of the vacant land just waiting for seed on Shorts' Point. Orchestrating a long distance agreement with the absentee owners, in 1895 he began farming again in earnest.

He built a modest house on the property and broke ground that year, spending his Fall hunting bighorn sheep and mountain lion[16] or prospecting in the mountains near the property. Gellatly was the first staker of the 'Heather Belle' mine back of Shorts' Point and according to his son John, he was also searching Shorts' Point for coal.[17] Coal can actually be found approximately two kilometers beyond the west meadow on the north slope of the property.

With the Spring of that first year, Gellatly began to concentrate on farming and taking care of his family which had now grown to a son and four daughters. He grew a variety of vegetables but mostly tomatoes and potatoes on the property and he was able to expand his production dramatically in the rich soil over the next two years. By 1897, Gellatly had enough produce in potatoes to consider selling some.[18]

The mining activity in the Kootenays seemed to him to be a logical market. After harvesting that year's crop with his crude 'go devil' (a primitive form of stone boat pulled by horses that was made up of a forked tree covered with planks) he delivered a full freight carload of spuds to J.B. Bruce's dock and the waiting SS Aberdeen.

"After the car was loaded and ready to go, the C.P.R. made the embarrassing discovery that no freight rate covering car-load shipments out of the Okanagan, existed.

"A hurried and frantic exchange of telegrams between the local agent and C.P.R. headquarters finally resulted in the settlement of a rate not particularly satisfactory to the producer, a rate based on the difference between the price of potatoes in the Okanagan and the price per ton at the car's destination - Nelson."[19]

With a total of nine children in need of an education and the nearest school many miles away, in 1896 the Provincial government agreed to open an 'assisted' school at Shorts' Point to teach the lower grades. The term 'assisted' meant the Province would pay a teacher the princely salary of $50 per month and provide a small grant for incidental expenses, so long as the parents provided a school room and other facilities and at least 10 children to attend the school.

Along with the children of their neighbours to make up the difference, the school had a total first year enrollment of seven boys and five girls. Gellatly, E.J. Wilson and B. Morden served as the first school trustees and hired William Sivewrite (he held a Second Class 'B' teacher's certificate) as the instructor.[20]

Shorts' Point school opened in September 1896. It continued to operate with Sivewright as the teacher in 1897 to the summer of 1898. The school didn't reopen again until January 1899 when J. Irwin was hired. The school trustee list was also revised to include D.E. Gellatly, N.H. Caesar and James Bruce. It went through a shortened school season and didn't reopen that fall because the Gellatly brood had been removed.

Gellatly had no mistaken understanding about his tenuous "renter"status at Shorts' Point, but he didn't likely anticipate his fortunes changing the way they did in 1899. The success of his vegetable farm convinced him there would be abundant value in the purchase of a Hoover potato digger that year, a modern machine capable of harvesting 3.2 ha (8 acres) of potatoes in one day.[21] Gellatly saw a future in vegetables and went as far as establishing a wholesale vegetable supply business from Shorts' Point when he arranged to ship two carloads of mixed vegetables each week from his farm and other market gardeners in the North Okanagan.[22] His plan was a good one, but during that summer everything fell apart.

Without warning, Gellatly learned that Shorts' Point ownership had changed hands. The new owner, R.N. Dundas, of Kelowna had somehow assumed the lease or title to the property Gellatly occupied and he wanted Gellatly to move immediately. Gellatly quite naturally objected. His business was just starting to blossom and he likely knew of Dundas. Dundas owned a small acreage in Kelowna where he was also raising potatoes and he had won prizes for three varieties of them at the Mission Valley Fall Fair in September 1897.[23] Gellatly's annual potato harvest was about to be underway. An umpire, Price Ellison, was designated in the legal dispute when Gellatly refused to move and Ellison directed Gellatly to vacate the property. It's assumed that date was November 24, 1899 because Gellatly also relinquished his role as the Bruce's Landing post master on the same day, and while it extended his tenure at Shorts' Point, it was not enough time for Gellatly to complete his harvest.

In anger about his treatment, which some reports claim was a reprisal by Ellison for an old slight about a horse, Gellatly searched the Okanagan for a piece of earth he could claim in his own name. Fifty kilometers (30 miles) south he found just that at Powers Flat near Westbank, a choice piece of property first pre-empted by Billy Powers in 1890.

Robert Napier Dundas arrived in the Okanagan in 1890 and like so many other young men, seemed to enjoy the rough and tumble lifestyle the valley offered. While he first settled in Vernon, it wasn't long before he migrated south towards Kelowna where in 1892-93 he purchased a 8 ha (20 acre) parcel of the Nicholson property which was being sub-divided for fruit farms by Vancouver developer G.G. McKay.[24]

Sometime during the summer of 1899, Dundas moved to Shorts' Point and immediately involved himself deeply in the local agricultural community. He planted peach trees on the property and by the end of September he had been elected as a director for 'Westside Lake' branch of the Okanagan and Spallumcheen Agricultural Society[25] and by January of the following year he'd assumed Gellatly's role as postmaster for the Bruce's Landing Post Office.[26]

It isn't until 1902 when a record appears for a land registry transfer on the property from Montagu and Hare and oddly it isn't to Dundas at all, but to a Sir John Poynder Dickson Poynder.

Poynder, the same age as Montagu and Hare, served as a British Member of Parliament for 18 years at the same time as Granville Hare. In 1910 he was titled as Baron Islington and appointed to the governorship of New Zealand. Fourteen years previous, Poynder had married Anne Beauclerk Dundas, the third daughter of Henry Robert Duncan Dundas of Glenesk, Midlothian, and grand-daughter of Robert Cornelis Napier, first Baron Napier of Magdala.[27] Baron Napier of Magdala (1810-1890) served briefly as Governor General and Viceroy to India in 1863 and has been honored with a plaster-cast of his bust in Britain's National Portrait Gallery.

The likelihood that the property was purchased for $5,000 by Dundas' brother-in-law is strong.[28] In a property conveyance dated October 12, 1903, title to Lot 686, less 12 ha (29.80 acres) was transferred to Murray McMullin. Seven months later, on May 12, 1904, the 12 ha that Poynder retained were conveyed to Dundas. This lot was at the mouth of Shorts' Creek.[29]

While it might seem that Dundas suffered the same displacement that had affected Gellatly before him, it isn't really the case. During the period between McMullin's purchase and his receiving title to the 12 ha, Dundas was busy building on his land holding. Dundas applied for a purchase claim on 156 ha (385 acres) of Crown Land up the hill behind the Shorts' Creek delta, surveyed as Lot 2920 in September 1903. After paying the Crown $319, he received grant to the property on June 24, 1904.

An article in the Thirty-ninth Okanagan Historical Society Report contains a description of Bob Dundas by Roger Sugars. Sugars arrived in the Okanagan as a child in 1905. He remembered Dundas as a tall and handsome man, well acquainted with horses. He "made a striking figure in his high-crowned Western hat and black angora chaps," says Sugars who looked upon him as something of a hero. According to Sugars' reports, Dundas taught the boy how to pack a horse for the bush and how to throw a 'diamond hitch'.[30]

Sugars' father, a trained school teacher, was engaged to instruct Dundas' children Nina and Duncan.

By 1905, the Dundas property contained the C.P.R. dock and the Shorts' Point Post Office, which had been re-established with the closure of the Bruce's Landing P.O. after Gellatly's departure. (Mrs. Dundas functioned as the post mistress from May 1, 1905 to June 16, 1905 and Bob Dundas picked up the task from August 1, 1905 to August 18, 1906[31]) Dundas used the C.P.R. dock as the point of export for the first fruit crop raised at Shorts' Point. In 1905, much to his apparent delight, Dundas sold a harvest of peaches from five trees for $100.[32]

In spite of his marginal success as a fruit grower, Dundas' tenure on the Shorts' Point property was rapidly drawing to a close by 1906 when ill-health prompted him to announce he would be uprooting his young family and returning to the 'old country'.

At a farewell banquet held in Dundas' honor, the local paper reported on Dundas' reluctance and regret.

Dundas was reported as "...saying that we was not going home, as some termed it who deemed him lucky; he was driven away by ill-health, which compelled him to live at a lower altitude, and by other reasons which he did not enumerate. He was going to a place of exile, for Okanagan was his real home. He was proud to be reckoned a Canadian by adoption, even if he could not forget Scotland, the land of his birth; and he hoped his children would always reckon themselves Canadians, as they were in fact. Should his health be restored in Ireland, he hoped to return to the Okanagan some day, a statement which evoked much applause."[33]

Dundas sadly sold his farmland to Louis Lailavoix, a man who had recently immigrated to the Okanagan from France with an older wife.

McMullin purchased Crown Grant Lot 2920 and Dundas made a huge profit.

McMullin was apparently a bachelor who lived alone with his Chinese cook in a large frame house on the property he acquired from Montagu and Hare for $15,000. It should be noted this is the same remote property that Shorts' tried to sell for $75 to no takers. While Dundas was staking out Lot 2920, McMullin was pursuing a 130 ha (320 acre) purchase directly west of the Dundas crown grant land, and had acquired it in September three years earlier. With Dundas' property, it gave him an estate of nearly 405 ha (1,000 acres) and McMullin began to make use of it as Dundas had foreseen.

Using the clear waters from Shorts' Creek for irrigation, McMullin planted 32 ha (80 acres) of Shorts' Point to fruit trees that included apples, pears, apricots, cherries, plums and 5 ha (12 acres) of peaches.[34] The influx of British immigrants to the valley made finding some help in the task fairly easy. McMullin hired two brothers, James and Walter Newton, and Walter's wife to assist in the Spring of 1906 but the wild country took its toll on them quickly. Forced to live on the property in an unaccustomed fashion (in tents), that summer the Newtons discovered how wild the west side of Okanagan Lake really was.

"...after a bear had rifled their provisions, the couple decided to pull out and they left brother James to plant the rest of the orchard."[35] Encounters with animals were still common along the west side of the lake. After all, the only land access was the old HBO trail, now overgrown and disused. It wasn't until 1916 that a rough wagon road was punched through the bush from Vernon to the Westbank ferry dock which provided access to Kelowna.[36]

Probably for a chance to profit and an opportunity to move from the remote location, McMullin sold his property on March 25, 1907 to Lieutenant-Governor James Dunsmuir for $35,000.[37]

Professor Ludovic "Louis" Lailavoix, M.A., for some years on the Faculty of Arts at the University of Paris, bought Dundas' acreage on December 19, 1906. Lailavoix had arrived in the Okanagan that summer claiming departure from France based upon religious persecution.[38]

"An air of mystery surrounded this suave young Frenchman, with his imperial beard and moustache, as he had no knowledge of farming or fruit growing. It seemed that there was no apparent motive for settling in this somewhat remote area of Western Canada, unless he was seeking a hideout."[39]

Lailavoix, who seemed to be around 35, had taken a woman who appeared to be in her mid-60s as a wife, a woman who seemed to have a drinking problem. It must have caused some general gossip in the region. According to a friend of the Sugars family, A.K. Menzies, he had known Mrs. Lailavoix under a different name as a wealthy widow living with her adult children in British Guiana. Like other stories of Fintry, the tales become embellished over time, shifting from fact to myth. The death of Mrs. Lailavoix is a case in point.

"...one cold night in the winter of 1907, one of the Shorts' Point ranch hands by the name of Harry Howis (who later settled in Summerland) arrived at our place on horseback and leading a spare horse. 'Would Mrs. Sugars please come with me to the Lailavoix house as Mrs. Lailavoix is very ill'. No doctors or telephones, so of course, my mother dressed in warm clothes and her heavy riding skirt and went with Mr. Howis. She found Mrs. Lailavoix to be unconscious and after a few simple tests she decided Mrs. Lailavoix was obviously dead. She reeked of alcohol and the remains of a bottle of wood alcohol was in evidence. Mr. Lailavoix explained that his wife had been drinking and run out of whiskey (or brandy) had found the bottle of wood alcohol and evidently swallowed most of it. Sometime the next day a doctor arrived from Kelowna or Vernon and rendered a verdict of death by alcohol poisoning. As simple as that! However, Mrs. Lailavoix's Will was in favour of her husband and it was quite substantial. Her grown-up family in South America fought the Will through the courts and won the case. Not long after, Monsieur Lailavoix left the country and has never, to my knowledge, been heard of since. There is a story that the old ranch house is haunted; perhaps Mrs. Lailavoix is still looking for the brandy bottle! The property was, apparently, heavily mortgaged in favour of Mr. McDonnell of BX Ranch in Vernon, who foreclosed as soon as Lailavoix departed. Was a bizarre crime committed or what? I leave it to you." [40]

While Mr. Sugars was undoubtedly repeating the story to the best of his knowledge, the accounts of her death in the Vernon News present a different history.

According to the newspaper, Mrs. Lailavoix succumbed after a heart attack on January 14, 1907.[41] Her obituary claims she was born in Hong Kong in 1875 which would have made her half the age Sugars suspected her of being. According to the obituary, she had been married to the Hon. S.J. Dare of Emerela, British Guiana. The prospect of grown children to contest the Will is impossible based on this information.

Lailavoix returned to France between April and July of 1907 when the property, heavily mortgaged in favor of a Mr. McDonnelly, was foreclosed.

In other instances however, Sugars' recollections seem accurate.

After Tom Hamilton returned to England to accept his inheritance, he was required to change his name to that of his benefactor. He returned to his horse ranch above Shorts' Point as an Attenborough, with a mousey new wife and a string of horses in tow. He immediately rebuilt his ranch house in a style more fitting his new-found wealth. *Photo courtesy B.C. Properties Ltd. collection.*

Tom Hamilton, the soft-spoken Englishman who took over E.J. Wilson's property is an example.

Sugars' remembers Hamilton's horse ranch being known locally as 'Rum Jug Canyon' because of Hamilton's apparent weakness for over-proof Hudson's Bay Company rum. In 1908 or 1909, it appears that Hamilton came into an inheritance and travelled to England. On his return to the Okanagan he brought with him a "charming but plain" English wife, a string of brood mares, two stallions, a new name and airs of superiority. Now calling himself Attenborough (a name he likely assumed with the inheritance), he proceeded to build a new log house to replace his old one, and a bunk house for hired hands. An industrious man, Attenborough built the first wagon road north from his ranch to Armstrong. The Attenborough Road still exists today.

What would have attracted the Lieutenant-Governor of British Columbia to purchase property at Shorts' Point? Dunsmuir at the time was one of the wealthiest men in British Columbia. From June 15, 1900 until 1902 he served as Premier and from 1902 until 1906 as the Lieutenant Governor. It's possible that he'd heard of the Okanagan's warm, dry summers often from his brother-in-law, Frederick Houghton.

Houghton had been a captain in the British Army who resigned his commission in 1863 and immigrated to B.C. On his arrival in Vernon, he applied for a B.C. Military Settlers Grant for 586 ha (1,450 acres) but this was reduced by the government to only 121 ha (300 acres). While living in Priest's Valley, Houghton became enamored with a beautiful Native girl, Sophie N'kwala, daughter of the chief at the Head of the Lake Indian Band. Allegedly, he married Sophie in 1871 and fathered two children with her. His memory seems to have failed him however, because after a trip to Victoria where he sought to appeal the decision on his grant application, he met Marion Dunsmuir (James Dunsmuir's sister) and seemingly "forgot" his family in the Okanagan. With Dunsmuir's direct intervention he managed to obtain his grant for 586 ha (1,450 acres) and created what is now Coldstream Ranch in 1872 which he later sold to the Forbes brothers. He married Marion in 1879.

Whatever the reason for Dunsmuir's interest in Shorts' Point, it persisted because on May 25, 1907 Dunsmuir also purchased Murray McMullin's acreage.

The acquisition was described in the press as having great promise.

"As instances of its productive power, it may be mentioned that last year Mr. McMullin picked three boxes of Flemish Beauty pears from two trees. There were no culls at all, and the fruit averaged 11 1/4 ounces. Mr. McMullin's peach trees are not bearing, but Mr. Dundas, whose ranch was situated on the same flat, received in 1905, $100 for the fruit of eight peach trees." [42]

Less than a month later calamity struck for McMullin. On April 11, 1907, it's suggested because of sparks from the chimney, the McMullin home and barn burned to the ground causing losses including furniture and private belongings estimated at $4000. Because the property was owned by Dunsmuir it made page one news on the coast.[43] But, it wasn't until June of that year that James Dunsmuir paid his first visit to the property with his daughter and son-in-law, Major and Mrs. Audain, in tow. Guy Mortimer Audain had given up his commission in the British Army to become Dunsmuir's aide-de-camp.

They spent a day and a half at the property before returning from Vernon in C.P.R. Superintendent Marpole's private railcar 'Brunswick'.

Dunsmuir seemed satisfied with what he saw in the Okanagan. He told the press he intended vast improvements to the property[44] and on July 3, purchased all of Lailavoix's property, buildings, implements and stock for $10,000.[45] He returned to Shorts' Point two months later in September with the Audains and his wife Laura Miller Dunsmuir. He planned to

"Byrdie's" Victoria mansion, paid in large part by the sale of the Shorts' Point property she received as a gift from her mother. *Photo courtesy B.C. Provincial Archives.*

stay for some time while Mrs. Dunsmuir convalesced and he oversaw the improvements he'd boasted earlier of undertaking but no improvements were made.

On October 17, 1907 Dunsmuir arranged for the title on the property to move into his wife's name, but she kept it only briefly, conveying the property to one of her seven daughters, Sarah Byrd Audain, on November 28, 1908. "Byrdie" and her husband Guy Mortimer never revisited the property again. Strapped with bills for the construction of their Victoria mansion 'Ellora' in spite of her father's wealth, she asked for nearly the amount the Audains needed to build Ellora and got it.

# Chapter Four Notes

1    Memoirs of the Earl of Listowel, 1996

2    Pakenham, T., *The Boer War*, Chapter 13

3    Doubleday, H.A. and de Walden, Lord Howard, *The Complete Peerage*. St. Catherine's Press, London, 1936 Vol IX: p. 112; The Dictionary of National Biography1922-1930, London, Oxford University Press, 1937: pp. 270-271

4    Doubleday, H.A. and de Walden, Lord Howard, *The Complete Peerage*. St. Catherine's Press, London, 1936 Vol IX: p. 85; Black, A. and C., *Who Was Who 1929-1940*, London, 1941: p. 814

5    Vernon News, March 17, 1892, p.5

6    Vernon News, July 21, 1892, p.1

7    Holliday, C.W., *The Valley of Youth*, Caldwell, Idaho:Caxton Printers:1948, pp. 230-232

8    Vernon News, November 15, 1894, p. 5

9    Vernon News, July 2, 1896, p. 4; Vernon News, November 12, 1896, p. 5

10   Vernon News, December 24, 1896, p. 1

11   B.C. Sessional Papers 1908, Report of the Minister of Mines, p. 128

12   Thirty-ninth Report of the Okanagan Historical Society, 1976, p. 55

13   Vernon News, May 16, 1895, p.5

14   Gellatly, D.H., *A Bit of Okanagan History*. Self-published. 1983, p 42

15   Vernon News, November 15, 1894, P. 5; Vernon News, November 21, 1894, p. 5

16   Vernon News, September 26, 1895, p. 5; Vernon News, November 21, 1895, p.5

17   Interview of John Gellatly by Imbert Orchard, 1965, tape in the Provincial Archives of British    Columbia, Victoria, Accession 1132-1; Vernon News, July 11, 1895, p. 5

18   Gellatly, D.H., *First Carlot to Leave the Okanagan*, Sixteenth Report of the Okanagan Historical Society, 1952, p. 128

19   Gellatly, D.H., *A Bit of Okanagan History*. Self-published. 1983, p 43

20   Annual Reports of Public Schools, British Columbia Superin

tendent of Education : 1895-1896, 1896-1897, 1897-1898, 1898-1899, 1899-1900

21   Vernon News, August 3, 1899, p. 5
22   Vernon News, June 8, 1899, pp. 4-5
23   Vernon News, September 23, 1897, p. 10
24   Kelowna Courier, September 12, 1896, p.1; Clement P., Kelowna Chronicles, Twenty-third     Report of the Okanagan Historical Society, 1959, p. 142
25   Vernon News, September 28, 1899, p. 8
26   Melvin, Post Offices of British Columbia, p. 16
27   Doubleday, H.A. and de Walden, Lord Howard, *The Complete Peerage*. St. Catherine's Press, London, 1936 Vol XIII: p. 115; The Dictionary of National Biography 1931-1940, London, Oxford University Press, 1949: pp. 719-721
28   Victoria Times, April 2, 1907, p. 6
29   Weeks, Captain J.B., *Steamboating on Okanagan Lake*. The Sixth Report of the Okanagan Historical Society: 1935, p 225; Victoria Times, April 1, 1907, p. 6
30   Sugars R., *Westside Story*, The Thirty-Ninth Report of the Okanagan Historical Society, 1975,     p. 54
31   Melvin, *Post Offices of British Columbia*, p. 111
32   Victoria Times, April 2, 1907, p. 6
33   Kelowna Courier, September 13, 1906, p.1
34   Victoria Times, April 2, 1907, p. 6; Victoria Times, March 28, 1907, p. 11
35   Johnson, M., *Oyama Pioneer Wrote Poems, Stories When Farm Homework Done*, The Twenty-first Report of the Okanagan Historical Society, 1957, p. 42
36   Sugars R., *Westside Story*, The Thirty-Ninth Report of the Okanagan Historical Society, 1975,     pp. 52, 61; Vernon News, *Marching Onwards*, October 21, 1937, p. 22
37   Victoria Colonist, March 27, 1907, p. 16; Victoria Colonist, March 28, 1907, p.1
38   Lailavoix, L., *Church and State in France*. Vernon News, April 4, 1907, pp. 3,7
39   Sugars R., *Westside Story*, The Thirty-Ninth Report of the Okanagan Historical Society, 1975, pp. 56
40   ibid
41   Vernon News, January 17, 1907, p. 5; Vernon News, January 24, 1907, p. 8

**42**   Victoria Times, April 2, 1907, p. 6
**43**   Vancouver Province, April 2, 1907, p. 1
**44**   Victoria Times, June 15, 1907, p. 5
**45**   Vernon News, August 1, 1907, p. 5

# CHAPTER FIVE
# THE MAKING OF A MILLIONAIRE

The same year that Dolman Shorts was born, across the Atlantic, in Glasgow a fortune that would eventually be used to pay for apple boxes, barbed wire and cattle was slowly being built by an enterprising young newspaperman.

William Dunn, the son of a miller in Fintry, Scotland, moved to Glasgow from his parent's farm in 1811 and joined the staff of the Glasgow Herald as a cashier.

His home had been a small village of about 300 in Stirlingshire, some 30 km (18 miles) southwest of Stirling and north of Glasgow in the Central Lowlands. Its a sleepy place, nestled in the green crook of rounded hills, and lies next to a trickle of water euphemistically called the Endrick River. The name Fintry likely derives from Geodelic Byrthonic as "Fionn" which means fair and "Tre" which means settlement.[1]

Evidence of habitation at Fintry extends back to the Bronze Age. Fintry Castle itself dates back to 1460 and the Laird of Culcreuch, named Andrew Galbraith, is mentioned in historical documents dated 1472. Records show the lands remained in Galbraith hands until 1622.[2] Culcreuch was the ancestral home and Clan Castle of the Galbraith chiefs from the 14th to the 17th century.

The parish was divided into two parts during the 17th century: Culcreuch on the west side up to the bridge at Gonachan and the farms on the east of the bridge. In 1622 the Culcreuch part was sold to Robert Napier (second son of John Napier of Merchiston and the inventor of logarithms). The property purchased by Napier included the south half of the Fintry hills and the farms surrounding it: the Spout of Ballochleam to

71

Culcreuch itself, comprising, apart from the policies and home farm, the farms of Easteer Glinns, Mains of Glinns, Craigend and Dalhillock, Rashiehill, Provanston, Over and nether Glinns, Knockraith, Killunnan, Bogside and the Jaw. The Napier family held the property for five generations before selling part of the estate, which included the farms of Craigton, Lurg, Spittalhall, Todholes and Carcarron east of Gonachon Bridge, to James Graham, 4th Marquis of Montrose in 1703.

The remainder of the estates, including Culcreuch Castle, were purchased by Peter Spiers in 1769 for £15,000. Spiers tried rather unsuccessfully to industrialize the area with construction of a cotton mill in 1796. While a success for 50 years it failed by 1844 and the village returned to its rural roots.[3]

Fintry, which looks much like the Okanagan, was not considered to be a place of beauty by the Scots. Rather, it was more the end of their tiny world as is evidenced by the fact Fintry was used as a large, barless insane asylum for some time.

"There was an unemployment problem from the second half of the 19th Century on into the 20th. One solution to ease the position was to house or foster imbeciles and Fintry became popular with the Authorities as an outlet. These poor folk were of some use, particularly on the farms, and payment to the "house" was 7 shillings per week. The idea that meat was bad for imbeciles was popular, and their diet was, for the most part, porridge and vegetables. The expression in Glasgow - "Och, 'awa tae Fintry" was not complimentary!"[4]

By the middle of the 19th century, the Dunns were established farmers on the ducal estates. They farmed Craigton, Spittalhill and the Lurg. Young William had a dream to change that.

William Dunn Jr. was a careful man who took to newspapering. For fifteen years, Dunn collected debts and kept the books for the small newspaper, becoming more familiar with the accounts and operation than even his employer. He moved up the corporate ladder from clerk to senior administrator, what we might now call a comptroller, and as the years passed he knew exactly where the pennies came from and where they went. His life is, in a way, a measure of the friendly, law-abiding nature of Glasgow at the time when you consider that it was well known Dunn carried the company's cash about with him in his pockets and yet was never robbed. Apparently, Dunn kept notes and sovereigns in one pocket and the lesser coins made up in packets of one pound each in another. He was a walking cash register. From this personal till, either in the office, on the street or in the tavern, Dunn paid the accounts to the newspaper's creditors and wages to the printers. As the publisher aged, Dunn saw a business opportunity.

In 1837 with partners Alexander Morrison and Robert Wardlaw, he purchased all of the company's stock for £3,000. In May of 1837 the partners contracted with George Outram, Advocate in Edinburgh, to become Editor of The Glasgow Herald.[5]

Dunn lived a life of solitude in modest lodgings above a bakery on Union Street for most of his life, remaining a bachelor until his death. He found his only joy in work at the newspaper and with visiting his three sisters. One in particular, Janet, appears to have been his favourite.

Janet had married David Waters, the owner of a small farming property known as Waterhead a few miles from where he grew up in Fintry.[6] The couple immediately had children and Dunn became the ever-present visiting uncle. He was particularly fond of his first nephew, David, and gifted 3.5 per cent of his holdings in the newspaper to the lad, eagerly bringing David into the business.

Also by 1840, Dunn had acquired solid control of the newspaper from his partners (of the 28 shares in the company, Dunn held 19, Alexander Morrison four, George Outram four and David Waters one) and he began considering how to divide his estate without having sons or daughters of his own to inherit.

He sold some shares to his brother-in-law's second cousin, a Glasgow commission merchant named Andrew Watters (not related) and in 1844 transferred a second share to David and two shares to another nephew Alexander Waters, who like his brother David was serving as a clerk in the Herald office at the time.

The history of the Waters brothers is a tragic one however. There were four of them: David, Alexander, William and James Coltart Waters. William died on July 15, 1844 followed on April 28, 1845 by his eldest brother David, within a year of receiving the second gift share from his uncle. David's two shares passed to his brother Alexander who died 12 months later on April 5th, 1846. The four shares in his possession were passed to the last surviving brother, James Coltart Waters, only 18 years of age at the time.[7]

A year later, almost to the day, Dunn sold two more shares to Andrew Watters and two others to John Cameron of the Londonderry and Glasgow Steam Packet Company, further spreading the wealth amongst his assorted relatives. Until 1854 the share register remained the same except for the sale of one other share to the new editor, James Pagan, who replaced Outram.

James Coltart Waters had acquired considerable knowledge of the newspaper in the four years following his inheritance, much to the pleasure of the aging Dunn who wanted to retire. In a clearly obvious act of nepotism, in 1854 Dunn appointed the 26 year-old to manage the company's affairs in association with George Outram, who was serving in an executive position.

While Dunn removed himself from active participation in the life of the newspaper, he didn't retire completely. Using some of his accumulated wealth, in 1860 he purchased the lands and estates of Craigton and Culcreuch, near Fintry, from the Duke of Montrose and was busy overseeing the construction of a mansion and mausoleum on the property. Showing a dry sense of humor that seems to have been genetic amongst the Dunns, he ordered windows installed in the mausoleum as a personal joke and as an obvious reminder to the common farming folk in Fintry of how far he'd climbed from the mill wheel.

When asked about why he ordered the windows, he's reported as replying: "Won't it be fine to look out on resurrection morning and see you poor Fintry folk trooping by!" as if he, because of his wealth, might not be among them.[8]

By 1860 the mansion was built but he never moved there. His declining health was the probable reason because instead, he lived with his sister at Bridge-end farm. He died less than a year later on May 15, 1861. Though his sisters Margaret and Jean, and his nephew James Coltart Waters were to inherit his wealth, it took six years before the estate was settled because all were "jointly interested in both heritable and moveable estate", which may have been a gentle way of describing a prolonged situation of legal hair tugging.[9] However, on July 8th, 1867 the quibbling about finances was resolved and a final settlement achieved. The sisters both took up residence at Bridge-end Cottage in Fintry and the mansion house was passed to their nephew, James Coltart Waters.

As a result of his inheritances, James Coltart Waters estate and holdings had become considerable. He had not only the Fintry property but also six shares of the newspaper and he controlled the shares owned by his aunts through the family trust that Dunn had set up. However, like his brothers, his life span was tragically short and he also died at a young age, passing on September 11, 1867 in his 39th year.

Waters had been married twice, his first wife dying at Bournemouth in 1857. His second wife, Grace Elizabeth Godwin, survived him by 28 years and gave him three children: Alexander William Dunn Waters, Grace Godwin and James Cameron. The convoluted passage of the Dunn wealth continued to the eldest male, Alexander.

James Cameron was born in Torquay, England on November 28, 1864 and was but three years old when his father died. He was raised by

Culcreuch Castle was the ancestral home and Clan Castle of the Galbraith chiefs from the 14th to the 17th century. Dun-Waters purchased it and the surrounding estates from the Lady Spiers.

his mother on the family estate at Fintry and though she tried to ensure that he took an active involvement in the agrarian business of the estates, he was still indulged as a fatherless child. In his youth, the closest he got to farming was strolls on shooting jaunts and hikes to go fishing. He grew to love nature and enjoy the freedom of the outdoors. It marked him for the remainder of his life. The estate lands were ideal for fishing and shooting with grouse, partridges, snipe, woodcock, hares, rabbits, pheasants and roe deer abundant. In the Endrick River, he was able to catch salmon and trout were plentiful in the Culcreuch Loch. At the age of 18 in 1882, he was sent up to Jesus College, Cambridge. With his wiry physique he excelled in sports if not academics, and won medals in both rowing and rugby.[10]

James Cameron lived the life of the well-heeled British gentry at Cambridge but little other than the athletic medals mark his passing there besides a Scottish eccentricity he began to cultivate. At the age of 21, his brother Alexander also had died and with that untimely passing, the entire estate then passed to the last remaining male in the family.

As was tradition at the time, inheritors took the name of their benefactors as a means of carrying on the family name. To succeed to the wealth, James Cameron Waters was officially required to adopt his great-uncle's surname. Dunn had wanted his family name to continue, but so did young Mr. Waters as the last surviving male in his own branch of the family. In a clever maneouvre, James Cameron acceded to the requirements of the inheritance by legally changing his name to James Cameron Dun-Waters, dropping an "n". The strange spelling became a life-long albatross with his name being recorded every conceivable way in surviving legal documents on both sides of the Atlantic.

A wealthy eligible bachelor, J.C. Dun-Waters found himself to be a prized marriage candidate both in Scotland and England. With encouragement to generate a male successor for the family fortune, two years later he married a well-bred young woman named Alice Orde. Alice was, without doubt, the love of his life, though J.C. didn't let that necessarily preclude the occasional dalliance as was often rumored later in his life.

Dun-Waters had become thoughtful and enjoyed seclusion even as a young man, and he took to the life of a landowning gentleman and publisher with relish. It gave him opportunity to organize and see his plans bear fruit, to hob nob with the titled and the gentry in England as well as Scotland, to hunt and fish at will and to make friends with those whose careers were contributing to development of the Empire. He spent his time between his estate lands in Fintry, the newspaper in Glasgow and rented accommodation in the west of England.

By 1887, the share structure of the Glasgow Herald reverted back to the 24 parts that it had been in Dunn's era, with James Cameron Dun-Waters holding six shares of his own and controlling three more in the family trust. Along with the Morrison family shares to dominate partner meetings, Dun-Waters' will was law in the day-to-day operation of the paper although he rarely interrupted or caused policy to be altered in the paper's editorial stance.

Instead, the young man who was just 26 at the time, used his wealth to expand on his land holdings. In 1890 he paid Lady Home Speirs £58,000 for the 2 428 ha (6,000 acres) in the Culcreuch estate, which included the castle that still stands there.[11]

"He was a 'character' in every sense of the word and 'knew' his tenants on the estate," and lived the life of a squire. A keen curler, he also supported the Fintry Curling Club financially. Dun-Waters name appears in the minute book of the curling club as a president and later a patron. It was formed in 1874. When Craigton Pond was frozen over, soup and "refreshments" were brought down from the Big House. His support continued in small ways for years. Even after he'd left for Canada, Dun-Waters sent £25 to John Welsh (a local carpenter), to build a hut at the pond expressly for housing stones and other equipment."[12]

But he didn't limit himself to life in rural Scotland.[13] He enjoyed the life in the south too much and made his primary residence Lutwyche Hall in South Shropshire, which with Scot frugality, he simply rented. In South Shropshire, the hounds became his avocation for a time and his prowess as a hunter earned him the title of Master of Fox Hounds of the prestigious South Shropshire Hunt in 1898.[14]

As he grew older however, he found the operation of the estate farms limiting and the repetitious detail required there to be tiresome. Although the hunting parties he organized were a pleasant diversion and well known throughout the area, life at Fintry was simply not diverting enough for a man of action and youthful energy. The Fintry farms were primarily devoted to sheep and cattle, most of the cattle were Aryshire. The valley floor was the

A young Alice Orde married into one of Scotland's wealthiest families but did not distinguish herself with a list of charitable works as was common to women of the gentry in her time. She was quiet and retiring. A perfect foil for Dun-Waters' eccentricity. *Photograph courtesy of O'Keefe Historical Ranch archives.*

only arable land, its production was limited to potatoes, turnips and grain so farming at Fintry was mostly spent waiting for crops that were invisible until the harvest. Dun-Waters was evidently bored by Fintry and gradually he began to look at the estate as a summer cottage more than his home, in spite of his family's history there. An example of his attitude can be seen in how he turned Fintry into a rest area for his horses and fox hounds. He sent his hunters to Fintry for their "summer holidays" where they were stabled on the Mill-lade. Hound puppies were also brought up from the South and lodged at farms to be "walked" by the tenant farmers.[15]

After his mother died in 1895, Dun-Waters felt even less hold at Fintry. He finally decided to unburden himself of the property at the turn of the century and he posted an extensive sales brochure detailing its' availability for sale. The brochure included a list of everything from

Dun-Waters' skill as a horseman quickly earned him the title of Master of Fox Hounds in the South Shropshire Hunt. *Photograph courtesy of O'Keefe Historic Ranch archives.*

furniture to the income received from tenants and is still posted with his name as owner in Culcreuch Castle.

In 1901 the property was sold to Walter (later, Sir Walter) Menzies and Craigton, including the farm. Bridge-end went to John Power of Comrie.[16] With part of the funds from the sale he purchased Plaich Hall, Church Stretton in 1902 and moved to Shropshire as his permanent home. Interestingly enough, Plaich Hall was once immortalized by "Ripley's Believe It Or Not". The ornamental chimneys of the residence in Much, Wenlock, England were constructed for its owner, Chief Justice Sir William Leighton, by a mason whom he had sentenced to die. Immediately after the completion of the chimneys, the man was returned to prison and hanged.

The decision to move to Plaich Hall created some business problems for him on other fronts.

Dun-Waters control of nine shares in the Glasgow Herald gave him 37.5 per cent ownership of Outram Press and enormous wealth in terms of the times. To increase the capitalization of the company and that wealth even further, on July 1, 1903 Dun-Waters led the other shareholders in conversion from a partnership to a private company. When it became a private liability company in 1903, capitalization was £300,000 meaning Dunn-Waters personal assets in the newspaper stood at £112,500.[17] He played an active role in strengthening the financial resources of the Herald, and was a regularly attending member of the Board, but his heart was not really in it either. He much preferred the outdoors, and he found

Dun-Waters, less than six-feet tall and wiry, cut a fine figure in his riding gear. The size of the outfit, contained in the Dun-Waters Collection at O'Keefe Ranch, hardly matches the 'larger than life' Scot's reputation. *Photograph courtesy of the O'Keefe Historical Ranch archives.*

himself pursuing his hobby of sport shooting more and more of the time. In 1908 it was that hobby that brought him to Canada.

Middle-aged, Dun-Waters was more adverturous than most men of his age. Tales of wild game in western Canada lured him to leave his wife with her companion and sail across the Atlantic in search of hunting trophies. He had a distinguished guide for at least part of the journey in Albert Henry George Grey, 4th Earl Grey.

Like Dun-Waters, the 4th Earl was a colourful character, involved in a great variety of activities and interests and their lives had many things in common. He started his career as a Liberal M.P. in the British Parliament in 1880 but lost his seat as a result of his opposition to Gladstone's Home Rule Bill of 1886. Similar to Dun-Waters, he managed his uncle's estates (3rd Earl Grey) for a time and was involved in the British South Africa Company until he returned to Parliament as a member of the House of Lords when he succeeded his uncle to the earldom in 1894. In 1896 he became Administrator of Rhodesia and on Dec. 10, 1904, the Governor-General of Canada.

Lord Grey took a leading role in movements such as co-operation and co-partnership, temperance (public house trusts), electoral reform (proportional representation), church reform, university extension, garden cities and, above all, imperialism (imperial federation, Dominion House). However, he is most famous for two things: his participation in the 1904

Plaich Hall was filled with family treasures and included the beginnings of Dun-Waters' prodigious collection of stuffed animals that he began to gather on various safaries to exotic and distant locals around the world. *Photograph courtesy of the O'Keefe Histocial Ranch archive.*

Alaskan boundary dispute with the United States and the donation of an elegant silver cup as a trophy for the Senior Amateur Football Championship on June 1, 1909.

The settlement of the Alaskan boundary dispute led to the set-up of the International Joint Commission and the Department of External Affairs.

The boundary between Canada and the Alaskan Panhandle, the narrow, jagged strip of land and islands that cut northern B.C. off from the sea, was not clearly defined when Grey assumed the Governor-General's mantle. The original boundary was vaguely set out in 1825 in a treaty between Russia, then the owner of Alaska, and Great Britain. When the United States purchased Alaska in 1867, it felt no urgency to examine the accuracy of the border provision of 1825, but when gold was discovered in the Klondike region of the Yukon in 1898, it suddenly took notice. Canada wanted a route to the Pacific as access to the Yukon and claimed Skagway as part of its territory. President Theodore Roosevelt thought otherwise.

In 1903 the dispute over the boundary was referred to a joint commission of six officials, three from the U.S. and three appointed by Great Britain. As Governor-General in 1904, Lord Grey inherited part of the diplomatic mess. Roosevelt had privately informed the British of the verdict he expected - and warned if it didn't happen he might have to send American troops to conduct a survey of the boundary. Teddy's stick was a big one. To maintain peace with the U.S. the British gave in to Roosevelt's demands and Canadians reacted in loud protest over the result. While historians seems to agree that Americans did have the stronger claim, Canadians were annoyed at the process. A lasting result of the dispute was the feeling among Canadians that Great Britain had served its own interest - conciliating the United States - at the expense of Canada. Many expressed the conviction that Canada could look after its own welfare properly only if it obtained the power to conduct its own foreign policy.[18]

Governor-General, Lord Grey, was one of the men considered to have betrayed Canada in his lifetime but remembered fondly today for a little gesture - the Grey Cup. Such is history.

Never rich, Lord Grey made continual attempts to improve his finances by investment in all sorts of concerns, usually ending disastrously. One such was a fruit ranch in the Kootenays and it was here Dun-Waters got his first taste of British Columbia.

After learning of the hunting to be had in the Okanagan, and the fact that Shorts' Point was more-or-less a gateway to the best hunting territory, following in the footsteps of the Hon. John Walter Edward Scot-

A modern photograph of Fintry, Scotland clearly shows the similarities in countryside between Dun-Waters' childhood home and the land stretching along Okanagan Lake.

Douglas-Montague and Richard Granville Hare Viscount Ennismore, 18 years earlier Dun-Waters decided to take a look. He bought a steamer ticket and on seeing the delta, instantly fell in love with the property that was soon to become his new home.

Locals who remember the first appearance of Dun-Waters have a different story to tell.

"Dunwater (sic) turned up with blue denim pants and a torn shirt and somebody wondered if he shouldn't be had up for a hobo.

"Jimmie Campbell was running the ferry at the time. Dunwater beat him down in price to take him to Short's Point and then pick him up in a day or so."[19]

By his own report however, "...when he first saw Fintry it was owned by a retired army officer. Capt. Dunn-Waters (sic) tells that, although he coveted the estate at once, he was too shy to enquire if the owner would part with it. Later, his agents arranged the sale, and here the Scottish sportsman settled himself, not with the object of farming for profit, but of development for himself the kind of estate in which he would take the maximum of personal enjoyment."[20]

On October 5, 1909, Sarah Audain agreed to sell Shorts' Point to the wealthy Scot for $22,500 and the property became Dun-Waters' on November 4th.[21] Calculating the purchase price based upon the Consumer Price Index, it is interesting to note that the value of goods purchased for one dollar in 1909 would require spending $17.00 in 2000. In other words, the $22,500 property acquisition might seem a bargain at today's values, but computed against the CPI that would mean an equivalent purchase of $382,500. It was a relatively enormous amount for a spit of land that had barely been improved.

Returning to Shropshire, Dun-Waters began to plan his future. The newspaper was doing well without his meddling and he described the potential of the agricultural economy waiting to blossom in the Okanagan to Alice as an adventure. Despite his age, 44, he felt a new sense of purpose. "Ach, potential for profit's enormous," he likely told his wife, "and the hunting, Alice! The hunting!"

# Chapter Five Notes

1    Wilson D., *The Story of Fintry*, c. 1975, Fintry Scotland, Fintry
     Community Council, p 1
2    ibid, p 2
3    Rev. D.H. Gerrard, Parish of Fintry, in *Third Statistical Acccount
     of Scotland: Vol. 18 — The Counties of Stirling and
     Clackmannan* ed. R.C. Rennie and T. Crowther Gordon (Glas
     gow:   Collins, 1966), pp. 214-217
4    Wilson D., *The Story of Fintry*, c. 1975, Fintry Scotland, Fintry
     Community Council, p 15
5    *The History of the Glasgow Herald*, Private, p 20
6    ibid, p 26
7    ibid, p 28
8    Wilson D., *The Story of Fintry*, c. 1975, Fintry Scotland, Fintry
     Community Council, pg 4
9    *The History of the Glasgow Herald*, Private, p 34
10   Vancouver Province, October 17, 1939, p 22
11   Wilson D., *The Story of Fintry*, c. 1975, Fintry Scotland, Fintry
     Community Council, p 5
12   ibid
13   ibid
14   Vancouver Province, October 17, 1939, p. 22
15   Wilson D., *The Story of Fintry*, c. 1975, Fintry Scotland, Fintry
     Community Council, p 5
16   ibid
17   *The History of the Glasgow Herald*, Private, p 58
18   H.H. Herstein, L.J. Hughes, R.C. Kirbyson, *Challenge & Survival:
     The History of Canada*, Prentice-Hall of Canada, ltd.
     1970, pp. 309-311
19   Hayman, L., *Captain Len's Ferry Tales*, p 6
20   Long, E.D., *Fintry in the Okaganan*, Canadian Homes and
     Gardens, Vol. 8, No. 5, May 1931,      p 28
21   Redmayne, J.S., *Fruit Farming on the Dry Belt of British
     Columbia: the Why and Wherefore*, 4th ed. London: Time Book
     Club, 1912, p. 108

# CHAPTER SIX
## THE LAIRD ARRIVES

What made Dun-Waters decide to give up on Great Britain? Why would he turn from the life of luxury and privilege at Plaich Hall for what would undoubtedly be a harder life in the Colonies?

Why did anyone at the time? The Thompson, Cariboo and the Okanagan received a steady stream of well-born, well-educated British settlers from the 1890s to the 1920s, known as 'gentlemen emigrants'. They were British public school boys, retired military officers, university graduates and aristocrats. There are no readily accessible records of the actual number that settled in Canada but by the late 1890s it has been estimated that nearly 27 per cent of the British adult male settlers were 'gentlemen emigrants'.[1]

Promoters of the time were describing the Okanagan Valley as a "Garden of Eden"

"Some people maintain that the Garden of Eden was located north by west, north from Mount Ararot (sic). Others differ-the point is open to argument. But anyone who has ever visited the Great Okanagan Valley which extends southward from Larkin across the international boundary, will agree that it might well have been situated in that beautiful, rich, rolling country."[2]

Perhaps Dun-Waters fell victim to the hyperbole of newspaper writers in Great Britain who picked up the promoters' drum and beat it regularly. The men who came to see for themselves were often wealthy and they had "edge" to them. They were men of vision and grit who helped tame the country. Dun-Waters was, in his own way, no different.

His eccentricity was, even then, well known. In fact, many decades after his death he was so fondly remembered for it back home that a writer for the Times of London wrote: "The Scot, especially the Highlander, sometimes can with great charm play the resplendent eccentric. There is a faintly barbaric streak in the splendour...Jim Dun-Waters...was such a Scot." [3]

Dun-Waters' affection for the outdoors, and his 'do it my way and damn the rest' attitude were probably the driving reasons for his decision to move. He carried the taint of his wealth with him everywhere reluctantly and Canada might have seemed a place where he could drop that pretense.

Before uprooting himself, he notified the Board of Outram Press of his plans. While he hadn't at that point decided to sell his shares in the company, it was clearly obvious that if life worked out as he hoped, he would never be returning to Scotland or England as a permanent resident. In a gesture typical of Dun-Waters, to mark his transition and thank the workers at the paper for their contribution to his wealth, in 1910 he distributed a bonus among the staff. The farewell gesture was substantial at £50,000 (using the rate of exchange in 2000 and the CPI, the same value of bonus today would require a gift of nearly $2-million). [4]

His decision to move also required him to give up his position as Master of Fox Hounds in Shropshire, which he did that May. He received a parting gift from the Hunt in the form of a silver statuette of a fox hound and a sundial. (The pedestal for the dial still stands in the garden of the Manor House although the dial itself has disappeared. One side of the pedestal had a brass plate inscribed with: "This sundial was presented to J.C. Dunwaters (sic) on his resigning the mastership of the South Shropshire Hounds in May 1910 by his friends and admirers in the County". On the opposite side of the dial another plate was inscribed with the following poem (authorship for the work was not declared on the plate but it is assumed it was written by one of the membership:

While the pedestal still exists in the gardens outside the Manor House, the sundial presented to Dun-Waters has long since disappeared. Its whereabouts are unknown. *Photo courtesy of O'Keefe Historical Ranch archive.*

*"Serene He stands among the flowers*
*And only marks life's sunny hours*
*For him dark days do not exist*
*The brazen-faced old Optimist."*

After the property sale was finalized, Dun-Waters made arrangement to hire his cousin James. The cousin on his mother's side was son of General Sir Charles Godwin and in Dun-Waters' likely estimation a good candidate for manager of his new estates. James Godwin had been involved in farming at Durban in the Natal Province of South Africa, another "wild" part of the world. He was familiar with the bits and pieces that had to be pulled together to establish an estate and apparently was willing to do so with the proper encouragement.

Because he had no child of his own with Alice, he turned to James as his selected heir. 'Come to Canada and manage my new estate James, and I will bequeath you my fortune when I'm gone. Help build your inheritance,' he may have said. Apparently James saw the logic in the plan.

With him James brought some learned habits that today

One of Dun-Waters' first acts as the new owner of the delta lands of Shorts' Creek was a hunting trip. A diary in the O'Keefe Historic Ranch archives describes his walk from Fintry beyond Kamloops and his disgust with the guide's handling of the horses. It presents a dramatic juxtiposition between the hunter and the animal lover that Dun-Waters truly was. *Photo courtesy of O'Keefe Historic Ranch archive.*

might be termed 'racist baggage' and unfortunately Dun-Waters hadn't considered how much of a wedge it would represent in his relationship with his heir. Dun-Waters was not the type of man who judged another by color or race. In Fintry, Scotland he willingly befriended the tenant farmers and worked alongside them, making every effort to improve their lot in life. His appraisal of an individual was made by the man's conduct and nature as can be clearly seen in a diary he kept of his first hunting trip after the purchase in which he considered fighting a guide for beating a horse and befriended a Metis guide's helper. This isn't to mean Dun-Waters ever forgot the status wealth had given him in society or that he eschewed its trappings. Just that on a personal level he looked at the man and forgot about his wallet.

James apparently couldn't see past the color of skin however, which

A steam-powered bulldozer was brought to the property by barge to assist in the logging operation.

Logging was also conducted across the delta using horses and mules.

And finally, the logs were cut to a uniform size on a portable mill. *Photographs courtesy of O'Keefe Historic Ranch archives.*

might have been understandable in the context of South Africa's settlement. James was used to the cheap and compliant labour force made up of Blacks and Orientals in Durban and reverted to the closest version of 'colored' labourers he could find in the Okanagan — Oriental immigrants. Godwin hired a substantial number of Chinese, Japanese as well as workers from the Indian sub-continent to man-handle the development of the Short's Point property for his employing cousin.

At the time, it caused a sizeable amount of resentment among local residents. Anti-Oriental prejudice was high in British Columbia as White settlers saw a rising tide of Oriental immigrants sweeping across the Pacific and feared inundation of able workers willing to labour for starvation wages and displace White workers from their jobs. [5]

Godwin did hire White men to manage the crews. Crawford Twiss, a teamster for example, was hired to work the orchard about 1910.

"I used to drive the team in the orchards. We used to cultivate the or-

Dun-Waters took great pleasure in pulling stumps single-handed. When horse-power was not convenient, he purchased a stump-puller for his exclusive use. *Photo courtesy B.C. Properties Ltd. collection.*

chards and collect all the apples and do all the spraying and the work in the orchards all the year 'round, naturally....

"There were two other teamsters there, bar myself, and we had a crowd of Japanese who picked the apples and one thing or another...

They used to get a couple of pruners there from Kelowna in the pruning season who used to go through and do all the pruning. We didn't have to do all the pruning; we had enough to do looking after the orchards without tackling the pruning. Besides, that wasn't our line — we weren't

An ingenious network of suspension bridges and flumes were built from wood milled at Fintry to transport water from Shorts' Creek for irrigation. Access however was not for the faint of heart. *Photograph courtesy of B.C. Properties Ltd. collection.*

This scenic shows the delta with the first few years of fruit tree plantings. Note how the different orchards were separated with mowed pathways that workers were required to use. *Photo courtesy O'Keefe Historic Ranch archive.*

pruners, or course."[6]

By 1912, Dun-Waters was already expanding the size of his estate by another 545 ha (1,346 acres)[7], which he had named after his Scottish home - Fintry. The property adjacent to his purchase on the lakeshore (Lot 2923) had been pre-empted by James Baxter Bruce in the 1890s but at the beginning of the century it was abandoned. Dun-Waters acquired it for the price of the back taxes and named it 'Craigend'. In 1909, Dun-Waters had acquired the property to the north of this land, Lot 2550, but disposed of it in a sale to James Muirhead. Perhaps Dun-Waters had a soft spot for the recent immigrant who hailed from Denny, a town very near Dun-Waters' Scotland home.

About the same time, Dun-Waters saw the need to properly irrigate the orchards if he wanted to maximize his crop yield and make his estate the model operation he desired. "To begin the development, Dun-Waters followed the example of other settlers in the valley by building an irrigation system to establish an orchard. Using the natural water supply on his property, Shorts Creek and a hundred foot waterfall, an elaborate irrigation system of flumes and pipes along with two suspension bridges to support the pipes were constructed not only to supply water for the orchards but to also power an electric generator which provided power for the entire estate. With the irrigation system completed, a 40 ha (100 acre) apple orchard was planted[8] The system required two suspension

This photograph, circa 1917, shows an early version of the Packing House and the S.S. Okanagan berthed at Fintry taking on a load of fruit. *Photo courtesty B.C. Properties Ltd. collection*

bridges to support the wooden pipes. With this gravity-fed water, Dun-Waters had 150 pounds per square inch pressure which was enough for him to install sprinklers and he became one of the earliest orchardists in the valley to use this method of irrigation rather than open-ditch style.[9]

Within two years of acquiring the Bruce property, Dun-Waters looked elsewhere for more land. Thomas Attenborough's property up Short's Creek represented a good location for cattle and hay production so he acquired it in 1914 and renamed it the Fintry High Farm.

Dun-Waters began regular hunting sorties into his new domain and quickly acquainted himself with the anachronous 'Old Man Love' who had a mine several more miles from the Attenborough property towards the headwaters of Shorts Creek.[10]

At some point during the First World War Dun-Waters also purchased Lot 3849 which had been known locally as Cedar Swamp, from J.E. Sugars for $1000 and the Sugars moved to Salmon Arm.[11]

In a fashion reminiscent of his time in Scotland, Dun-Waters relied on his manager to run the estate, but on occasion participated in the farm labour. Dun-Waters, it was reported often, didn't put on airs. He was just as likely to be seen in dungarees held at the waist by a rope as he was in any other attire. One such "visit" to physical labour was recalled by Crawford Twiss.

At the time, Godwin had men digging ditches and two new farm hands were joined one morning by an older, but evidently fit fellow. He took to the pick and shovel without complaint. It was a hot summer day under the relentless Okanagan sun and the two younger workers soon began to transfer their frustration with the rock and gravel to their employer, a mysterious Scot they had never seen. Amongst themselves they complained about the work and the pay offered them for the effort. No doubt, on a rest break from the back-bending chore they gazed north at the 'big house' and compared bilious assumptions about the owner who was at that moment probably sitting in the shade sipping something cool. Both men concluded the Scot have probably never soiled his hands with honest labour but regularly dirtied them counting his money.

The farm hands rested in the ditch, assured of being hidden from view until Godwin appeared.

"We're in for it now," they might have said to each other as Godwin strode towards them, but when he passed and stopped instead at the older man to ask permission on some detail of the Fintry operation, they were flabbergasted. Dun-Waters apparently approved Godwin's request, looked at the two workers and just smiled. It was typical of the private jokes he enjoyed playing on the unsuspecting.[12]

While he was a gentleman, schooled in proper conduct, Dun-Waters was also known to forget the strict decorum of his upbringing. Twiss recalls:

"You'd be sitting in his sitting room 'round the fire and he'd probably come in late from some of his pursuits. He'd walk right through the sitting room there with a towel around his waist...to the bathroom. He says: 'I know you people don't mind.' He says: 'We've all seen birthday suits before, but I'm going to have my bath.' He wasn't at all bashful in anything he did."[13]

In the early years, the Fintry fruit crop was the primary focus of endeavour, although Dun-Waters also maintained a small herd of Herefords on the old Attenborough property and he ran a herd of approximately 100 brood mares.[14]

Twiss remembered how Dun-Waters was particularly fond of clearing land. Perhaps it was seeing the land made arable and productive that pleased him. In fact, he enjoyed the process so much that to allow him the individual satisfaction of clearing land on his own, he purchased a Creston Stump-puller. The device enabled him, by use of leverage, to work a stump out of the ground singlehandedly.

"That was his main hobby — to have a wonderful finish when he pulled out the stump that he'd been pulling."[15]

In 1911-1912, after a year living in less than sumptuous quarters left on the property by Dundas, Dun-Waters began to modify his living arrangements as well. Construction on Fintry Proper, also known as the

Fintry Manorhouse, began.

Dun-Waters used Kelowna stonemason, John Abbot Bailey, who had also contracted for the installation of the innovative sprinkler irrigation system, for the construction.[16] Using granite quarried from the cliffs that edge the delta, the house was built in the style of stone farming cottages in Scotland.

"It was a spacious bungalow built of stone, quarried from the hillside of the estate that was used for the exterior and the massive interior fireplaces, and lumber that was shipped by the CPR stern wheelers which regularly stopped at Dun Water's (sic) pier. Also on the exterior, verandahs were extended along three sides of the house. The living quarters consisted of a sitting room (25x30ft) dining room, five bedrooms with fireplaces, a kitchen, three bathrooms and a cellar which he stocked with imported Thompson's Scotch whiskey." [17]

A visitor described the manor house later as having:

"...all the easy comfort of luxury; generous living rooms, halls and dining room, the gleam of mellow mahogany, old silver, antique brass, priceless product of master craftsmen of former days, brought out by Capt. Dun Waters (sic) from his Scottish home. Reminiscent also of his earlier days are pictures of foxhounds and horses." [18]

The new environment Dun-Waters was creating for his enjoyment gave him room for his eccentric nature to run. He cared little about the opinion others in the area may have had for his desires or his antics, as is illustrated in this recollection by R.J. Sugars:

"He refused to recognize local customs. He rode English saddle in English britches and jodhpurs. He carried a hunting horn which he used to use — you'd hear this hunting horn through the hills and it was Dun-Waters out for a ride. He had a pair of bloodhounds and these things used to cause a little bit of hard feeling because they used to run deer. He didn't use them really to hunt with, but he'd go out for a ride and these bloodhounds would be with him and they'd pick up the scent of a deer and they'd run it, you see. Well, that was deeply resented by the old-timers who felt that the deer and the game were sacred. But he disregarded anything of that kind. He fenced his property in. He fenced across trails, which also made him extremely unpopular." [19]

A humourous anecdote again supports the myth of Dun-Waters enigmatic way of conducting his life. As the story goes, when Dun-Waters decided to fence his land he travelled to Vernon alone, dressed in the casual style of a workman or farm hand. In Dun-Waters' case, that probably included a rope belt and a torn shirt.

In Vernon he went to the largest hardware supply and approached the clerk inquiring about the price of barbed wire. The clerk, surveying the character of his customer by the clothes, put out feelers about his "credit".

Dun-Waters hadn't the time for such nonsense. In a huff he walked across the street to the competitor's establishment where he ordered his barbed wire without asking about price – the order was four carloads!

After spending some time in the store making other purchases he left, but forgot his jacket. Doug Campbell, the young man who served him, hung the jacket up in the stock room and thought no more of it. Weeks later when the Scotsman returned, Campbell returned the jacket.

Dun-Waters made a public point of fishing out his wallet and counting several thousand dollars onto the counter. Pleased with Campbell's honesty when the total matched his memory, he complimented Campbell to the gathered crowd of spectators and then, just as magnanimously, gave the boy a reward - 50 cents.

"One thing we all did in those days was hunting - for meat. We shot a deer or two and we ate them all winter. He treated hunting as a sport. He was a sportman in the full sense of the word. He was a big-game hunter and he hunted for trophies. He employed guides and a full-time taxidermist. He hunted all through the country.

"But at the same time he was an extremely kind man in a peculiar way. He provided a great deal of work for many, many people. He developed that farm. He put in a complete electric light system (and a private telephone exchange for seven telephones). He put in a complete irrigation system. Dun Waters (sic) didn't concern himself with the management of the ranch. He liked to be the man behind the manager. The manager did everything as far as the ranch was concerned."[20]

The fencing was more an inconvenience to neighbours than anything, but fencing was only one bone of contention the locals had with the Scot. Employment of Orientals gave definite offence as well, as did his forceful personality. Public meetings at the Ewings Landing schoolhouse were long remembered by the locals at which Dun-Waters engaged in loud and vociferous arguments with Mrs. Hollick-Kenyon, a cultured English-woman who had settled there as Dun-Waters neighbour in 1909.[21] British emigrants across the province had been fomenting angry racism against the Asian menace for some time. Newspapers in Vancouver, Victoria and Nanaimo openly played to the fear mongering, but Dun-Waters didn't care. In fact he hired a Chinese cook and a Chinese man servant and developed such a strong friendship with his Oriental workers that he had his will amended in 1938 to include a $1000 gift to one of them! Dun-Waters probably also felt he had to maintain the strong familial front and support his manager's hiring practices. Regardless, he approved of Godwin's management style in public and fenced his property completely and worse still, he expected that line of barbed wire to be respected. Light-hearted trespassers were not tolerated even years later as an anecdote about two young men who had been to Kelowna to play tennis illustrates. The youngsters, residents at Ewings Landing, decided to stop at Fintry one day. It is likely they never made that mistake again.

"They were returning one evening by boat, from Okanagan Land-ing. Somewhat the worse for wear they missed Ewings and landed at Fintry. Now, Mrs. Dunwaters (sic) had on the beach a small house in which she kept certain necessities, including her bathing suit. Our friend became inspired with the idea of donning this garment and going in for a swim. Just at that moment, however, Dunwaters (sic) appeared on the scene, gun under his arm and dog at his heels. He took a dim view of such desecration of his wife's apparel. Our friend was obliged to remove it, and encouraged...to make his way home, clad only in the suit nature pro-vided. It is not recorded whether he walked or rowed." [22]

While on the property, there was no question as to who the owner was. Dun-Waters had no compunction about firing farm hands on the spot if they broke his rules. However, when he left Fintry to hunt, he seemed to change. He took on a role of student, quietly trying to learn the tricks of the best hunting guides he could entice to take him into the mountains.

To extend his time in the bush Dun-Waters, built himself 'way' cabins high in the mountains on range leases he eventu-ally acquired. He hired expert Indian guides and wandered the province on horse-back, travelling northward as far as Alaska in search of big game trophies. So prolific at bagging game was he, that during the winter he hired his own full-time taxider-mist, G.L. Pop, of Vancouver, to stuff and mount his trophies. Pop, who ventured north to Alaska with Dun-Waters, eventu-ally became a prominent furrier in Van-couver.

It was on that trip to Alaska when Dun-Waters learned of the war that had broken out in Europe. [23]

The call to come to the service of

At the age of 50, Dun-Waters joined the Middle-sex Yeomanry. *Photo-graph courtesy O'Keefe Historic Ranch archive.*

95

Dun-Waters trained troops in France, Italy and Egypt. *Photograph courtesy of O'Keefe Historic Ranch archive.*

his homeland with mobilization in August 1914 was a strong and urgent one for Dun-Waters even though he was 50 years old! As part of the British Empire, Canada was pulled into the war and the Borden government began to muster volunteers immediately, but men over 'fighting age' were discouraged from participating.

Committed to overcoming this age impediment, Dun-Waters evidently left Canada as soon as he could, vouchsafing his estate to the hands of his manager, Godwin.

When he'd arrived in England, Dun-Waters somehow managed to secure himself a commission as a Second Lieutenant in the 1st County of London Middlesex Yeomanry.

On January 17, 1917, at the age of 53, he "intimated his resignation from the board"[26] of the Outram Press giving the fact he was participating in the Great War as his reason. He probably also wanted capital for his investment in the Okanagan, and at the time freely admitted that Canada had become his new home, and it was a home to which he intended to return after the conflict.

Dun-Waters served for a short time on the staff of Sir Roger Paget, a personal friend of his which may account for the army's willingness to accept such an old recruit (Dun-Waters was the godfather to Paget's children) . For the most part however, Dun-Waters worked in the supply corps as a training officer, spending time in Italy, France and Egypt. His personal training manual, archived at O'Keefe Historic Ranch, shows how Dun-Waters applied the skills of a hunter to teaching the task of sentry.

It was only in Gallipoli where he saw action however and he was wounded for the first and only time. Strangely , the Army List maintained by the Public Record Office in Kew Gardens has but one listing for Dun-Waters as an active soldier in December 1915 when he was made an Honorary Lieutenant and received the Silver Star War Badge.[24] Other than that, record of his name does not exist save for a microfilm copy of a fire-damaged award report which lists his service beginning March 1915 and ending with discharge in January 1918.[25]

Curiously, he was bestowed the Silver Star, a medal that normally was 'given to cover the bullet holes on the boys who were shipped home'. Traditionally, that medal was awarded only to the enlisted men and was therefore 'beneath an officer'. According to the National War Museum in London, for an officer to receive such a medal was usually out of the norm, indicating that Dun-Waters had evidently made a point of receiving it. Such receipt would have quickly ostracized him from

Inspite of his age, Dun-Waters demonstrated the proper techniques for transport of equipment in the field. *Photo courtesy of O'Keefe Historic Ranch archive.*

other officers however. Immediately following the award he was decommissioned from service with the rank of Captain on the basis of age and his wound.

Dun-Waters decided to stay and continue to serve in his own way however. Contacting his wife Alice, he decided that a 'hospital' was needed for 'the lads' in Alexandria.

Photographic evidence of this 'hospital' shows a group of grass huts in the sand. While diplomatic dispatches from Egypt to the Home Office in London during this period seem to go into incredibly specific detail about all the goings on of British nationals in Cairo and Alexandria, no written account seems to have been made of Dun-Waters' magnanimous gesture. Not even the English newspapers of the time, which often had to detail bridge tournaments to fill their columns with local color, mention the hospital or the Dun-Waters. It can only therefore be concluded that the 'hospital' was more of a convelescent home or respite place for soldiers. Nonetheless, Dun-Waters and Alice, assisted by Katie Stuart, spent the remainder of the war there, operating the facility with

Dun-Waters 'hospital' was actually a series of grass huts, but they served the intended purpose and provided hundreds of soldiers with a necessary period of care and recuperation. *Photograph courtesy of the O'Keefe Historic Ranch archive.*

funds he supplied.

Before the war ended however, Dun-Waters removed back to London and Glasgow.

The War years had taken a toll on his health. Pictures show him aged, and bent, leaning on a cane. However, throughout the war and at a distance, and in spite of his resignation from the Board, Dun-Waters still maintained an influence on development of the *Glasgow Herald* indirectly. During those years he campaigned amongst the former partners, now all major shareholders, to broaden their wealth (and his) by taking the company public and by 1920 it was registered as such. According to written histories of the newspaper, the sudden rise in foreign ownership of the Scottish newspaper alarmed many of the original owners however. For a century from 1783, control of the company had been in the hands of Scots resident in Scotland but after going public that ownership structure changed with 53 per cent of the share capital of the company resting in the hands of non-resident owners. More than once it had been necessary for the Chairman and other members of the board to travel to London when important matters had to be settled. Dun-Waters felt directly to blame, but his stake in the company had grown to £304,778 (in Canadian dollars at rates of exchange at the time of writing, it would amount to liquid cash assets of about $6 million). So, he followed through on his 1917 resignation in 1919, selling 1300 shares to William Hay and another 1300 to Henry Drummond Robertson. One hundred shares were sold by Mrs. Grace Godwin Sutthery (his sister) and her husband as well.

Now, swimming in cash from his investments and the sale, after the Armistice in 1919 Dun-Waters returned to Fintry with Alice and Catherine. 'Katie's' brother Geordie, who had been working in Ocean Falls as an

Following the war, Dun-Waters returned to Canada with his wife Alice (left) and her companion, Catherine Stuart (right). *Photograph courtesy of O'Keefe Historica Ranch archive.*

electrician, was soon recruited to join them as the estate accountant.

When Dun-Waters got back to Fintry with his extended family, it was clear that the Fintry Proper was too small to hold the new arrivals and Godwin's family as well. To solve the problem, Dun-Waters had a large two-storey Tudor-style house built for the Godwin family. This home, became known as the White House. However, the Godwin's style of management conflicted with a gentler nature Dun-Waters had acquired through the war. The 'new blood' on the estate in the form of Geordie and Katie, probably also influenced Dun-Waters as well. Katie, a warm and affectionate woman, decried the living conditions of the Orientals who were relegated to an area called 'Japanese Camp' on the north bank of

Wong Ying who provided valet services for the 'Laird'. *Photograph courtesy of the O'Keefe Historic Ranch archive.*

Short's Creek between Burnside and the dairy farm.

"Some of the Japanese employees were Ozumi, Sakakibara, Sasaki, Sugawara, Ouchi. All still well known families in Vernon,"[27] but Godwin was not known for treating them kindly.

Perhaps it was Katie's influence or some other more basic personality clashes, but the relationship between Dun-Waters and his cousin seems to have deteriorated rapidly on his return for whatever reason. Dun-Waters, flush with capital, continued to expand his holdings in the Valley. Within a year, with the purchase of DL 4690 (McMullin Creek) and other parcels, he had over 1214 ha (3,000 acres) accumulated as well as a sizable tract of Highland Forested Crown Land leased. The Crown Land extended south and west of properties operated by the Douglas Lake Ranch.

By 1922[28], Dun-Waters could take Godwin's style no longer and decided to sever his relationship with his younger cousin. Godwin (whose son's name can still be seen as graffitti in the octagonal barn) had his wife and two children with him at Fintry however. He too had purchased a small parcel of land on DL 2550[29]. Their parting was destined to be harsh. Godwin had, afterall, come half way around the world to be Fintry's manager. He expected a huge inheritance and had started to put down roots of his own in anticipation.

To make the break, Dun-Waters had to rely on cash. He paid Godwin $40,000 to leave the position of general manager.[30] The agreement also meant that Dun-Waters was cancelling Godwin's inheritance. In 1999 dollars, the severance payment would have been equivalent to slightly more than $400,000.

Not one to do things half way, Dun-Waters had the 'White' House (since destroyed by fire) and Burnside built for the Pym brothers. When Ronald Pym found Burnside too large, Dun-Waters had a bungalow constructed. Later known as the 'Gate House' it is located at the Park entrance. *Photograph courtesy of B.C. Properties Ltd. collection.*

With Godwin sent packing, Dun-Waters quickly accepted two brothers: Guy and Ronald Pym, to manage the estate on his behalf. Guy became the ranch manager and lived in the White House built for Godwin while Ronald managed the orchard operation. A second brick house at the north side of the mouth of Shorts' Creek, and named Burnside, was built for Ronald. Ronald found Burnside too large for his single lifestyle and the upkeep troublesome. He was moved to a cottage built at the foot of the mountain on the south side of the creek. This house, more recently called 'The Gate House', was later occupied by Mr. and Mrs. Wilf Potter, who managed the farming operations at Fintry from 1964 until its sale to B.C. Parks.

Other changes to the Fintry estate operation were made after the War as well. To diversify a little, Dun-Waters began clearing the trees from the High Farm he'd purchased from Tom (Hamilton) Attenborough, to make hay meadows. During this period, he employed more than 200 men in clearing the land with horses. By 1923, the fields were home to a herd of 300 Hereford cattle. Either ranching was too difficult in the post-War years or the Pyms were not up to the task. That year all but 75 of the

Herefords had been sold and the Fintry estate operation chalked up losses of $50,000. To put this enormous loss in context, that would have meant a one year loss of $500,000 in current coin. Not even Dun-Water's wealth could sustain such failure for long.

The Pyms left Fintry on April 1, 1924 under stormy circumstances with criticisms that Guy spent too much of his time cultivating affairs with female neighbours instead of orchards and that Roger was equally poor management material with a gin bottle always at hand.

This time Dun-Waters turned to Angus Gray. Gray fell in love with Fintry too and avidly took to the duties of general manager. He served in that position for the next 24 years.

Gray moved into the White House with his wife and their children Ewen and Ishbel and Dun-Waters once again began to relax in a life of serenity.[31] Gray's skilled hand was evident. In the decade from 1927 to 1936, the Fintry or-

Angus Gray served as General Manager of Fintry for nearly a quarter century. Pictured left to right: Ishbel, Isabella, Ewen and Angus. *Photograph courtesy of O'Keefe Historic Ranch archive.*

chard produced an annual average of 22,000 boxes of fruit with many varieties no longer grown in the Okanagan. It had 5,020 trees with about two-thirds being apple.[32]

| Variety | No. of trees |
|---|---|
| MacIntosh Red | 910 |
| Wealthy | 940 |
| Delicious | 783 |
| Jonathan | 725 |
| Stayman Winesap | 345 |
| Rome Beauty | 315 |
| Winter Banana | 210 |
| Transparent Crab | 380 |
| Other Apple Varieties | 58 |

| | |
|---|---|
| Pears | 22 |
| Cherries | 215 |
| Various Stone Fruits | 117 |

A report on the condition of the Fintry operation by H.W. Evans, District Field Inspector, Department of Agriculture for British Columbia states:

"This orchard has been extremely well managed in the matter of all orchard operations, including soil maintenance, pruning, spraying and general care of the trees, and the greater portion of it contains trees of full bearing age."

"It was after the War that the more extensive development of Fintry was made by the owner. This involved a complete irrigation system for the 200 acres of bottom land; water for this purpose was obtained from Short's Creek."[33]

"A normal year will produce 12 tons of cherries, 25,000 boxes of crab apples and 15,000 boxes of several well-known kinds of high-grade apples," one report states.[34]

The Fintry crew were able to load a box-car full of apples a day during picking season. Pictured far right is Art Harrop. First in line is Angus Gray's son, Ewen. *Picture courtesy Art Harrop.*

To accommodate the production, Dun-Waters had a packing house built next to the wharf where the fruit was packed in boxes produced in his own sawmill. Fully-packed, each box weighed 18 kg (40 lbs). A marvel of the packing house was the automatic, power-operated fruit grader Dun-Waters had installed there. The boxes were hand-trucked across to the C.P.R. wharf and loaded onto a barge which was then towed away for delivery to the Associated Growers of British Columbia, Ltd. co-op in Kelowna.[35] At the peak of its production, the orchard operation at Fintry turned out a carload of apples a day during picking season.[36]

By this time, the Dun-Waters had also sculpted their residential corner of Fintry into a showplace and care of the many plants and gardens required the attention of a full-time gardener. Dun-Waters hired Andrew White for that task in 1922 and he had a house built for him on mountainside between the Short's Creek falls and the stock area that would soon also be home to the unique octagonal barn that still stands on the property.

The two-story log house overlooked the orchards and its high A-frame peak earned it the title of the"Chalet". Built by Peter Lawrence, a resident of Ewings Landing, with the help of Wallace Colquhoun,it had a massive fireplace in-side which was built by a man named Baird, who travelled in for the job from Enderby. The "Chalet" was victim to fire in the 70s, after much renovation and loving improvement heaped upon it by artist David Falconer.

The 'Chalet', built on the hillside above the octagonal barn, was lost to fire in the 1970s. It had a red roof that served as a landmark to boaters for decades. *Photograph courtesy B.C. Properties Ltd. collection.*

While raising Hereford cattle had proven a financial dis-appointment, it hadn't discouraged Dun-Wa-ters completely. He harkened back to his days in Scotland and the hearty, long-horned beasts that gave milk there. He developed a veritable passion for Ayrshires in the Okanagan, and was willing to lecture uninterrupted for hours on their superb character.

"He possessed a one-track mind and was proud of it. He was Scots through and through, and it was his delight, following a half-hour lecture on the virtues of the Ayrshire above all other cattle, to demand of his visitor why it was that dairymen the world over did not abolish other milking breeds, substituting the Scottish cattle for them."[37]

In his own words, the logic of Ayrshires in the Okanagan seemed obvious:

National champion producer - Bumblebee. *Photograph courtesy of O'Keefe Historic Museum archive.*

"The Ayrshire are Scotch cattle and good cattle so why should not Scotsmen in the country grow Ayrshire? Then, too, pure bred cattle are the only thing the Old Country farmer has to sell to this country, so why should not Scotch farmers in Canada buy them?"[38]

The Scot decided to put his money where his heart was. He began with inquiries to purchase the finest stock he could find in Scotland, and he also re-hired J. Honeyman, a Vancouver architect and old Cambridge school friend who had designed the White House, to build Fintry a show piece barn.

The structure Dun-Waters chose for his stock manager T.H. Baird to run was to become one of the few such octagonal barns ever built. Dun-Waters demanded that the barn be the ultimate in modern farm planning. All the 50 or so stalls were to face towards a central silo and circular manger. The design demanded that all the

Dun-Waters often had the Ayrshires photographed for sale and publicity purposes. *Photograph courtexy O'Keefe Historic Ranch archive.*

conveyer tracks in the barn be curved. Despite it's unusual format, the barn worked well.[39]

When getting cattle from Scotland proved to be not immediately possible, in June 1924 Dun-Waters solicited the help of George C. Hay,

District Agriculture officer in Kamloops, to purchase two milk cows, five two-year old heifers, a bull calf and a bull named "Chapmanton Indicator' from a breeder in Quebec.[40]

Dun-Waters wanted pedigree. 'Chapmanton Indicator' was a white and brown beauty born February 29, 1920. Bred by Hugh W.B. Crawford, of Chapmanton, Castle Douglas, Scotland, the bull was imported in May 1921 by R.R. Ness & Sons, Howick, Quebec for Erskine McOuat of Brownsburg, Que. The Canadian Ayrshire Herd Book of 1916 describes the reasoning for the breed among dairy cattlemen:

"The Ayrshire appeals to one as combining all the essential requirements of the perfect dairy cow...her broad and clearly defined forehead, with

The octagonal barn served as the hub to a group of farm buildings and corrals. *Photograph courtesy of O'Keefe Historic Ranch archive.*

wide-set upstanding horns; her medium length of clean cut face, slightly dished, showing veins, with full bright placid eyes, gives a countenance which denotes strong character. The open muzzle shows good lung capacity and the strong jaws ability to handle large amounts of food."[41]

But Dun-Waters, a man of poetic bent, was just as likely to quote a poem by a fellow breeder when he was describing the Ayrshire to potential dairymen the Okanagan:

*"But if, in the group of the milky way,*

Dun-Waters often opened the Armstrong Fair leading the pipers and was filmed by the NFB one such occasion. *Photograph courtesy of the O'Keefe Historic Ranch archive.*

> *There shines one star supreme,*
> *'Tis the bonny cow from Scotland's shore,*
> *The Ayrshire, the dairy queen."*[42]

Each year following, for the next seven, Angus Grey was sent east to the Royal Winter Fair in Toronto to expand the herd, and Dun-Waters initiated importation from Scotland to improve the breed in the Okanagan.

Acquisitions from the herds of the Earl of Stair in Wigtownshire and the Stewarty of Kirkcudbright were undertaken on three occasions with one being more than 40 cattle. Dun-Waters sold the bulk of these imports to other local Ayrshire owners. With the cattle, he often imported their keepers as well.

"A Mr. McBryde...came out to Canada with one of these consignments, and says he landed at Armstrong on June 12th, 1930, and stayed there for 21 days until after the cattle were all sold to the various buyers, then went down to Fintry to work for Capt. Dun-Waters."[43]

Dun-Waters was tireless in his efforts to promote the Ayrshire breed in B.C. He wrote articles for the newpapers and in 1929 even donated a small herd as a gift to the University of British Columbia[44] He also gave breeding stock to calf clubs and Farmers' Institutes in central and northern British Columbia in order to encourage proliferation of Ayrshires[45] and during the 1930s, annually presented a Fintry heifer to be won by a member of the Ayrshire Calf Club at the Interior Provincial Exhibition in Armstrong.

"To further attract ranchers to invest in Ayrshire, he convinced a number of Scottish Duchesses to award sterling silver spoons as a special Ayrshire prize for those ranchers who exhibited their Ayrshires in the I.P.E."[46]

According to the record of production lists, one such winner in 1934, Mildred Brydon, named her calf 'Cinderella'. The calf later placed as the lead in class for production among Ayrshire's in Canada.

British Columbia was not Dun-Waters only area of distribution when it came to the Ayrshires. In 1934 and the years that followed until World War Two, saw sales of breeding stock from Fintry finding their way to China, Japan, Shanghai and Hong Kong. But during his life Dun-Waters never made the herd operation at Fintry a huge one.

"By 1931, Fintry had a line-up of 130 Ayrshires exhibited at the

When Dun-Waters donated Ayrshires to the University of British Columbia, local Scots lined the streets to celebrate this example of pride in an export from the 'auld' country. *Photograph courtesy of O'Keefe Historic Ranch archive.*

Tons of manure were recycled to the orchards and pastures on the estate. *Photograph courtesy B.C. Properties Ltd. collection.*

Interior Provincial Exhibition at Armstrong. This was the largest show-ing of Ayrshires ever in Western Canada."[47] The official records of the Breeders' Association don't seem to agree however. From his first ship-ment until Fintry was assumed by the Fairbridge Farmschool for Boys, there were rarely more than 71 Ayrshires registered with the Breeders' Association documents as owned by Dun-Waters. In some years, when he was most avidly distributing the cattle amongst other breeders, the stock level they recorded dropped to only 3 or 4 and in the few years afterwards rarely exceeded 14, but they were of the highest quality. Every cow at Fintry could comfortably produce 4 536 kg (10,000 pounds) of 4% milk and they often placed with distinction in the provincial produc-tion records.[48] In fact, 'Fintry Honeysuckle' is listed in the Canadian Ayr-shire Breeders' Association records as the nation's top producers for two years in a row with 8 583 kg (18,922 pounds) of milk and 416 kg (918 pounds) of butterfat testing 4.8 per cent in 1936 and 8 819 kg (19,442 pounds) of milk and 428 kg (945 pounds) of butterfat testing 4.46 per cent in 1937.[49] 'Alloway Miss Crummie', during a 305 day test in 1928, produced 5 399 kg (11,903 pounds) of milk and 252 kg (557 pounds) of butterfat to make her the top producer in the province that year. 'White Lily', another Fintry Ayrshire, placed as second.

With that kind of productive volume, Dun-Waters had to find mar-kets and he did it with the C.P.R. steamers that plied Okanagan Lake and

Fintry was a regular place for visitors from around the world, but by the early 1920s Alice was finding it difficult to entertain. This photograph shows Alice relaxing in the garden with Katie (kneeling) and Lady Baden-Powell. *Photograph courtesy of O'Keefe Historic Ranch archive.*

with the co-operative creamery in Vernon.

But while Dun-Waters began the new venture in 1924 at the age of 60, other parts of his life came to a sad close.

On May 1, his beloved 'Missus' finally passed away from a stroke. Her life-long companion, Catherine Stuart recorded the event in a small calendar diary.

"***Monday, April 28th*** *— We came in late for dinner. Missus had a stroke 8:00 p.m.. Doctor came 12:30 and Miss Wood, sat up all night.*

***April 29th*** *— Missus just the same. Wood left and Miss Brown came. Doctors Arbuckle and Logie here for dinner. Lovely day. Master cut the grass and got very hot and tired.*

***April 30th*** *— Much the same. Had Mrs. Gray over for the night. Poor old dear had a very troubled night. She wanted him to rub her which he did many times during the night.*

***May 1st*** *— Going on just the same. Sleeps a good deal. Miss Cherry arrived. Doctor and three ladies here to tea and we thought she was better and going to get well, but she went to sleep about 6 p.m. and died at 9:15 — never having woke up.*

***Friday, May 2nd*** *— Nurses left. We buried our dear in the garden at 6:00 p.m. Rev. Gibson brought Mr. Lloyd down. Duckering, White,*

*Gray, Brand and we three (Dun-Waters, Katie and Geordie)."*[50]

The 'Missus' grave still exists in the garden outside the Manor House at Fintry. Originally Dun-Waters picked the spot as the one she often relaxed at in her chaise lounge, and he had dark red, scented roses planted there in a bower. The headstone erected there does not illustrate the wealth he had at his fingertips. It is not large and monumental as is seen so often of headstones erected in grave yards. It is a simple hunk of stone found on the property, and inscribed strangely with *"Here lies my dear Old Missus in her garden. 1924, J.D. Dun-Waters"* and not her name or specific date of death.

For a time the bower was maintained and until at least 1943 it carried a copper plate on the wooden arch up which the roses were entwined. A visitor to the property that year recorded the inscription as:

*"Go thou thy way and I will go mine,*
*    Apart yet not afar;*
*Only a thin veil hangs between*
*    The pathways where we are.*
*And God keep watch 'tween thee and me.*
*    This is my prayer.*
*He looks thy way, He looketh mine*
*    And keeps us near;*
*I know not where thy road may lie*
*    Or which way Thine may be.*
*If mine may lead through parching sands*
*    Or thine beside the sea;*
*Yet God keep watch 'tween thee and me*
*    So never fear*
*He holds thy hand, He claspeth mine,*
*    And keeps us near."* [51]

After the 'Missus' died, it seems that Dun-Waters reverted to being even more thoughtful and turned to his hunting as a regular past-time rather than an occasional enjoyment. That Fall, Katie wrote to William Hay (one of the men to whom Dun-Waters had sold his stake in Outram Press) to report on the 'old Master's health' and a close call during a blizzard when Dun-Waters eschewed the danger to track a wounded deer.

Hay replied on December 9, 1925 to Katie saying he was happy that Dun-Waters still found the energy to hunt.

"So the Master had got his Deer alright (sic). There is a lot of walk and hunt about him yet although I see you find he gets more easily tired.

"So you can all get lost after all and within 400 yards of home."[52]

While the 'Missus' was living, Katie served as her full-time companion and upon her death she seems to have transferred herself to Dun-Waters. With her brother Geordie, the three shared the same house. Dun-Waters many stock investments normally required him to travel to Vancouver to attend to that end of his business. On June 20, with Katie travelling with him, he left the estate in the hands of Gray who was also overseeing workmen hired to build an addition to the south side of the Manor House. Dun-Waters had long been collecting his hunting trophies and he'd decided to place them in a suitable showplace environment.

The addition, to be his trophy room, was just beginning to rise when he left. Just a week later, on June 27, for some unknown reason smoke was seen billowing from the attic in the Manor House. While Dun-Waters knew of the history of house fires at Fintry, and had invested in fire fighting equipment to prevent a similar tragedy from happening on 'his watch', he hadn't taken into consideration the fact he might be away when fire occurred. The workmen, unfamiliar with the equipment, were forced to watch the smoke and ring the alarm bell that would call farm hands in from the fields. It took the men 15 minutes to arrive.

With presence of mind, the construction workmen were able to rescue some furniture, paintings and stuffed animals while they waited, but most of the homes furnishings were lost to the growing conflagration. By the time the farm hands arrived, the construction workers had cut a hole in the roof and the equipment was used to douse the fire. Working together in teams, the men managed to save the new addition, but sadly the main

After Alice's death Dun-Waters and Katie often spent weeks in the back country camping and hunting together. 'Dunny' guts a kill as 'Bunny' looks on. *Photograph courtesy of O'Keefe Historic Ranch archive.*

To house his hunting trophies, Dun-Waters decided on an addition - a Trophy Room. *Photograph courtesy B.C. Properties Ltd. collection*

To build the extension, Dun-Waters used granite quarried on the property as he had done for the Manor House itself. *Photograph courtesy B.C. Properties Ltd. collection.*

A mysterious fire destroyed almost all of Dun-Waters' and Stuarts' belongings. While rebuilding, 'Dunny' and 'Bunny' lived in Burnside. *Photograph courtesy O'Keefe Historic Ranch archive.*

house was razed down to its stone walls and chimney.

Upon learning of the fire, Dun-Waters raced home. He surveyed the damage stoically at first, then rushed into the debris, madly kicking at burned timbers to reach a special spot in his former home. With a pick he dug in the ashes and located a trap door into which he disappeared for a few minutes before resurfacing, a bottle of wine and whiskey in his hands. His secret wine cellar had, much to his joy, been spared.

With his wife's death still fresh in his mind and the prized heirlooms that marked their life together destroyed along with Katie and Geordie's goods, Dun-Waters contemplated what he should do next. There was nothing to do but rebuild. He moved with Georgie and Katie into the vacant Burnside home.

By November it was done and loads of lavish furniture imported from Britain were moved into the freshly plastered rooms. Dun-Waters took the fire as an opportunity to 'remake' the Manor.

"When the trophy room was completed, the walls were decorated with heads of elk, mountain goat, buffalo, timber wolf and stags. In a special alcove a miniature mountain gorge was reconstructed, complete with rocks, a waterfall and in the centre, mounted in a lifelike pose, was an enormous black bear that Dun Waters had killed." [53]

In actual fact, the prize exhibit in the grotto was the 1 270 kg (2,800 pound) Kodiak bear Dun-Waters had bagged on Kodiak Island in the Aleutians. Kodiaks are distinguished by their large size, light-brown colour, high shoulders, massive wide heads and shaggy coat. They are the largest of all flesh-eating mammals living on land. Dun-Waters had taken Pop, his taxidermist, with him on the trip specifically in order to give the bear the correct initial treatment once it was shot.

Designed to house his treasures in 'natural' surroundings, he imported a green carpet for the floor of the Trophy Room at a cost of $1,000. It was an enormously expensive sap to his ego then, that would have cost $10,000 if laid on the floorboards today.

"The front of the house was meticulously landscaped in lawns and gardens which led to the lakeshore. At the back of the house was a set of stone steps, "the looping stone", used by guests for mounting their horses.

"When the estate was completed after the War there were two houses for the managers, three guest cottages, a barn, several outbuildings including a packing house and a curling rink. The ranch also included pig sties and a pighouse and a granary. Later a shed was built for farm machinery, a blacksmith shop and an ice house." [54]

*(**Editor's Note**: In the years that followed, Dun-Waters insisted on preparedness by all the staff at Fintry in the event of fire. Even into*

115

*the 30s, Art Harrop recalls how Dun-Waters would periodically rouse all the staff at 3am with a ringing of the fire bell "to see how fast we could respond".)*

D un-Waters also took the opportunity of the reconstruction to re-plenish his horde of alcohol and imported $5,000 worth of Hill Thompson of Leith Scotch Whiskey privately marked with his own "Laird of Fintry" label. Pictures of all sorts hung on the clean walls and antiques of the finest quality were arranged for comfort. He had more "trophies" than he could mount in his "trophy room" and various animals and birds lurked from corners and doorways eve-rywhere.

One in particular brought Dun-Waters great joy. A black bear he had killed was stuffed and mounted in a menacing pose and stored on the porch. On the occasion when Dun-Waters had guests for din-ner, the 'fresh meat' was also treated to a liberal post-meal libation or two along with tales of dan-gerous creatures he had hunted in the hills sur-rounding Fintry. When the visitors were ready to take some air, Dun-Waters would nonchalantly lead them with their glasses charged out to the verandah and then happily watch the startled outbursts as they encounted the bear in the darkness.[55]

Dun-Waters had developed quite a reputation among other Valley residents when it came to the lavish hospitality of his evenings and the liberal pouring of his private-labelled whiskey. His image was so famous that non-drinkers were known to skulk about the estate when they came to visit friends for fear they might encounter the Laird. It was a better choice, it seemed, than offending Dun-Waters by refusing a friendly drink.[56]

As has been previously described, Dun-Waters joy was hunting in the outdoors and he maximized the remoteness of Fintry for that pursuit, combining his own property with several thousand acres of grazing rights around it[57] which he also acquired. In a sales brochure he developed, Dun-Waters included a specific roster of the type of game in the area and the length of time it took to locate it:

| | |
|---|---|
| *Elk* | *4 to 5 hours* |
| *Bear* | *1 to 8 hours* |
| *Cougar* | *1 hour* |
| *Mule Deer* | *15 minutes* |

Inside the Trophy Room. The bear cave is on the immediate right. *Photograph courtesy of O'Keefe Historic Ranch archive.*

A cave was built in the Trophy Room to house Dun-Waters' stuffed Kodiak bear. *Photograph courtesy of the O'Keefe Historic Ranch archive.*

Dun-Waters kept four back country cabins fully stocked for his trips with all the comforts of home - including an ample supply of his private label scotch whiskey. *Photograph courtesy B.C. Properties Ltd. collection.*

| | |
|---|---|
| *Coyote* | *10 minutes to one hour* |
| *Spruce Grouse* | *3 hours* |
| *Blue Grouse* | *30 minutes to 2 hours* |
| *Pheasants* | *2 minutes* |
| *Quail* | *1 minute*[58] |

Until his death, Dun-Waters made annual hunting trips into the back country of Terrace Mountain where he had built several cabins for hunting bases. According to an article in the Vernon News, Dun-Waters enjoyed the tranquility of the woods.

"The late Capt. Dun-Waters was a firm believer in the value of reflection. Annually he made extensive and arduous excursions into the mountains both behind Fintry and the country round it. He had cabins back in the hills where at times he dwelt in solitude reflecting on world trends, the movement of peoples and other matters of historic import. He would hunt sufficiently to keep himself fit and return to his home refreshed and reinvigorated."[59]

Like so much else about him, his habits formed myths amongst the locals. Hunting was no different. Several texts claim, without proof, that Dun-Waters imported California Big Horn to the Terrace Mountain area solely for the purpose of hunting. Not true, or at least not proved.

According to Orville Dyer, a wildlife biologist with the Ministry of Environment, Lands and Parks, the California Big Horn were endemic to the area. The grasslands from the Okanagan to Kamloops appear to

118

have been part of an extensive migration corridor used by the Big Horn and the Shorts Creek population was likely part of a bigger population extending to Mount Boucherie in Westbank. Encroachment of the grasslands, predation by hunters and ranchers who wanted the Big Horn destroyed to avoid disease amongst their domestic sheep, all contributed to the dramatic depletion of Big Horn seen today.

In fact, in the 1990s wildlife biologists had identified 50 in the area. The number remaining today has not been determined exactly.

As he got older the sport of hunting took much out of Dun-Waters and the trips in the back country necessarily became less difficult and shorter. The winter of his wife's death, Dun-Waters started to pass more of his time in an other sport he'd practiced in Scotland: curling.

The first Fintry curling rink was made that winter by diverting water from Short's Creek near Burnside onto a patch of level ground. A 'proper' rink was built near the barns the next year with a roof and electric lighting for throwing the rocks well into the evening. At the time, to curl actively meant serious discipline. The competitive circuit included Vernon, Armstrong, Salmon Arm, Enderby, Revelstoke, Kelowna and in some years Penticton (if the weather was cold enough for ice in the southern reaches of the valley).

Dun-Waters spread his enthusiasim for the sport to Armstrong, where he became an avid member of a club he helped form. The local press was happy to report the official opening of the Armstrong Curling Rink on February 10, 1931 with an end by end account of the first 'visitors' game. Dun-Waters, accompanied by Jock Reid, Geordie Stewart and Angus McKay took on a rink skipped by John E. Jamieson, with Harvey Brown, W.A. Smith,R.M. Ecclestone as members.

The local rink won and though no score was recorded, the Armstrong Advertiser reported that "the Fintry curlers were somewhat handicapped in not having had too much opportunity to play for several seasons due to lack of ice".[60]

Whenever business took Dun-Waters to Vancouver during the winter, he made sure he had the time to play and occasionally challenged the locals with his "travelling rink". He gained so much notoriety with his play and generous donations to the Vancouver Club, Dun-Waters was eventually named an honorary club president. In fact curling drew him to Vancouver when anything else was ignored and he avidly participated in every Canadian Pacific Curling Bonspiel held in Vancouver, from its inception in 1932 until his death.

An untitled poem he crafted best describes his feelings for the 'roaring game':

Curling was done at Burnside outdoors until Dun-Waters' built his own two sheet curling rink next to the octagonal barn. *Photo courtesy B.C. Properties Ltd. collection.*

*When you're feelin kinda groggy*
*and the blues have got you down,*
*Just drop into the curling rink*
*and throw the rocks around.*
*It will drive away depression*
*when you make a chap and he,*
*And a straight one chips the winner*
*brings a twinkle in your eye.*
*And how it helps to sooth the nerves*
*that are all frayed and raw,*
*When your opponents are lying three or four*
*and you make the perfect draw.*
*And there's glory in a fast one*
*that comes through a narrow port,*
*There's in turns and out turns*
*and there's shots of every sort.*
*You cannot be a piker*
*and you must stand the gaff,*
*And learn to hit them with a smile*
*and miss them with a laugh.*

*Today you take a licking*
*and tomorrow in the game,*
*Your mates and your opponents*
*why they treat you just the same.*
*But the keenest joy in curling*
*to those who love it ken,*
*Is the fact that when you play it*
*you associate with men.*
*O there's games and other contests*
*to prove a sportsman's worth,*
*But to those who have the love and lesson*
*they're the finest sports on earth.*
*And when the last Great Skipper calls*
*to write against your name,*
*He writes not if you won or lost*
*but how you played the game.*
*So if you're feeling kinda groggy*
*and blues have got you down,*
*Just drop into the curling rink*
*and throw the rocks around.*

Dun-Waters made sure that new men being hired were asked two questions: Were they Catholic or Protestants; and did they have any skill with the broom. Being Scot of course, also helped.

One cold winter afternoon as several were waiting for him to show up in his tam and scarf, Angus Gray saw Dun-Waters walking from the house to the rink. Dun-Waters stood a moment at the edge of the trees enjoying the view and it struck Gray that the old man was like an old-time Scottish Laird surveying his estate. He called out to the other curlers in jest, "Aye lads, here comes the Laird of Fintry!" and the nick-name stuck (behind his back) to replace his former nom de guerre of Captain.[61]

Dun-Waters likeability seemed to

A pose from the skip. *Photograph courtesy O'Keefe Historic Ranch archive.*

121

Catherine 'Katie' Stuart as a young woman. *Photograph courtesy of O'Keefe Historic Ranch archive.*

soar as he played the role of Scottish Laird to the admiring audiences at the curling bonspiels and the Armstrong Fair. Such an impression was made by his vocal shouts and attire, the Vancouver Province made this note of it after his death:

"From opening day, the sturdy figure of the 'Laird' could be discerned at almost any hour in rough tweeds, a natty Scotch Tam atop his head, yards of red woolen scarf wrapped around his neck and trailing down his back, and trousers stuffed into overshoes from which peeped heavy red woolen socks.

"Inevitably, his glasses would be steamed over, and his seamed, kindly face would be a study in concentration as he planned the next strategic move of the game. From a red-mittened hand would dangle his broom.

In the heat of the game, his stentorian voice would boom orders while the Fintry aggregation of Scots would toil mightily with broom and rock."[62]

Art Harrop and his wife Marie, are among the few residents in the Okanagan who lived and worked at Fintry during Dun-Waters period. Harrop joined the Fintry crew in 1933 at the age of 19 as a milker, and he recalls how seriously Dun-Waters took the participation of his staff in his enjoyment. If they travelled to a bonspiel, they were compensated at full wages and equal time off when they returned home.

"Dun-Waters didn't associate with the men. Only at curling time. That's where I learned to curl. When we used to go out I was on the team. I was the lead and I had to do all the sweeping. Geordie Stuart was 3rd, Angus was 2nd and I was lead."

"I milked Fintry Honeysuckle for two years and she was givin' out 120 pound of milk a day. I'd milk her every four hours when I first went there and I never got a holiday for two years. I had to milk her because a change of hand and she'd go right down. In those days people didn't have holidays anyway. They didn't have coffee breaks either, though we used to have a smoke time."

For three years he did so until health problems forced him to transfer to the orchard operation. Art still remembers "the Laird" and Angus Gray as "a great bunch to work for". He enjoyed being part of Dun-Waters' competitive curling team, and on a few occasions he tended the horses on Dun-Waters' hunting trips.

"He was a good fella. One time he was walkin' down the road when the apples were on and we picked up this apple from the ground. It was a nice red Mac. He said throw that away and take one off the tree. That apple is to feed that tree for next year."

"You could walk up that road where you come down to Fintry, about 50 yards and look down and you'd swear a lawnmower had cut the tops of those trees. There wasn't a branch stickin'up."

That bit of homey advice is all Art remembers of Dun-Waters' orchard experience however. He says 'the old man' never worked the orchard. "Pete Scott ran the orchard and Dave Lawson was the foreman over everybody. Dun-Waters didn't associate with the men. Only at curling time."

In the years that followed Alice's death, Katie and Dun-Waters shared their lives like a maried couple might. They had pet names for each other, he calling her 'Bunny' and she him 'Dunny'. They often left Fintry for extended hunting and fishing excursions alone and the pictures they took clearly show they didn't set up separate tents.

It also seems that for public consumption at least, Katie maintained the 'master' and 'servant' tableaux. For friends however, it was clearly different.

In 1927, Dun-Waters first learned of the illness that would eventually claim his life. Upon telling Jean Furse of the prostrate cancer, Katie received a heartfelt letter of encouragement.

"I need not say take care of him," Jean Furse, wrote. "I know he is all your life to you and your life's care. Thank God he has you."[63]

Dun-Waters, it seems, didn't share the same feelings for Katie however.

# Chapter Six Notes

1       Koroscil, P.M., *A Gentleman Farmer in British Columbia's Garden of Eden*, 1991, p 89

2       Allison, H. B., *Another Eden Discovered in the West*, Provincial Archives of British Columbia, Victoria, BC

3       London Times, October 20, 1939 p 10

4       Vernon News, October 19, 1939, pg. 9; Vancouver Sun, Oct. 16, 1939, p1

5       Interview of R.J. Sugars by Imbert Orchard.

6       Interview of Crawford Twiss by Imbert Orchard, October 1965, tape in Provincial Archives of British Columbia, accession 794

7       Land Titles Office, Kamloops, BC

8       Interview of Crawford Twiss by Imbert Orchard, October 1965, tape in Provincial Archives of British Columbia, accession 794

9       Interview of R.J. Sugars by Imbert Orchard

10     Sugars, R.J., Westside Story, 50th OHS, 1976, pgs 51-62

11     Wolsey, J.K., *Muirallen Estates*, p. 154; Falconer, *Dun-Waters of Fintry*, p. 98; Sugars, *Westside Story*, p. 62)

12     Interview of Crawford Twiss by Imbert Orchard, October 1965, tape in Provincial Archives of British Columbia, accession 794

13     ibid

14     ibid

15     ibid

16     Gellatly, D., *Pioneering in Okanagan*, 39th OHS Report 1975, p. 93; editor's note to Clara Clark, *My Childhood Memories of Westbank*, 22nd OHS Report 1958, p. 15

17     Digney, E.F., *Dunwaters Family of Fintry*.

18     Long, E.D., *Fintry in the Okanagan*, Canadian Home and Gardens Magazine, 1931, p. 28

19     Sugars, R.J., *Bright Sunshine and a Brand New Country: Recollections of the Okanagan Valley*, 1890-1914 compiled and edited by David Mitchell and Dennis Duffy (Sound Heritage, Vol VIII, No. 3, Victoria, 1979), p. 10

20     ibid

21     Wolsey, J.K., *Muirallen Estates*, 36th OHS Report 1972, p. 155; Sugars, R.J., *Commodore Herbert Hollick Kenyon, COI*, 40th OHS Report 1976, p. 150

22     Wolsey, J.K., *Muirallen Estates*, 36th OHS Report 1972, p. 158

23     Vancouver Province, October 17, 1939, p 22.

24    Army List, December 1915, p 383
25    War Office Record /95/2729, 2730, London Regiment.
26    *The History of the Glasgow Herald*, Private, p 72
27    Digney, E.F., *Dunwaters Family of Fintry*, p 7
28    *Wrigley's B.C. Directory*, p. 225
29    Digney, E.F., *Dunwaters Family of Fintry*, p 4
30    Falconer, D.G., *Dun-Waters of Fintry*, p. 96
31    ibid, pp 96, 98
32    *The Fintry Estate (1937)*, pp 14-15:
33    Falconer, D.G., *Rambling in Paradise*, p 2.
34    ibid, p 3
35    Dendy, D., *Fintry* pg. 86 this information gleaned from interview by Dendy with Mrs. R.T. Graham.
36    Long, E.D., *Fintry in the Okanagan*, Canadian Home and Gardens Magazine, 1931, p 28
37    Vancouver Sun, October 17, 1939, p. 4
38    Digney, E.F., *Dunwaters Family History* p. 5
39    Interview of R.J. Sugars by Imbert Orchard.
40    Vernon News, June 26, 1924, p 1; letter from Angus Gray to Mr. Newton of the B.C. Ayrshire Breeders' Assn., July 19, 1949, in the Vernon Museum Archives
41    *The Canadian Ayrshire Herd Book*, 1916 pg xxxvii
42    *The Canadian Ayrshire Herd Book*, 1916 pg xli, J.L. Stansell, Styraffordville, Ont.
43    Wamboldt, B., *The History of S.O.D.I.C.A.* (Shuswap Okanagan Dairy Industries Cooperative Association) Vernon: Vernon News, 1965, p. 33
44    Ellis, M.G., *Laird of Fintry's Ayrshires*, Family Herald, August 9, 1930
45    Vancouver Province, May 20, 1947, p. 20 Industrial Section
46    Digney, E.F., *Dunwaters Family of Fintry*, p. 5
47    Falconer, D.G., *Dun-Waters of Fintry*, July 1974
48    Ellis, M.G., *Laird of Fintry's Aryshires*, Family Herald, August 9, 1930
49    Wamboldt, B., *History of S.O.D.I.C.A.*, p. 30; and Vancouver Sun, July 7, 1938, p. 10
50    Falconer, D.G., *Dun-Waters of Fintry*, pp. 96-97.
51    Sipprell, W.J., Western Recorder, Vancouver, September 1943, pp 4-5
52    Letter from William Hay, 88 West Regent St., Glasgow, Dec. 9, 1925

**53**    Digney, E.F., *Dunwaters Family of Fintry*

**54**    ibid

**55**    Falconer, D.G., *Dun-Waters of Fintry*, p. 97. The house is de
scribed on pp. 7-8 of *The Fintry Estate*, the sales brochure
Dun-Waters wrote to entice buyers.

**56**    Dendy, D., interview of Arthur Gellatly

**57**    *The Fintry Estate* p 12

**58**    ibid, p 5

**59**    Vernon News, October 19, 1939, p. 6

**60**    Armstrong Advertiser, January 12, 1967.

**61**    Falconer, D.G., *Dun-Waters of Fintry,* p 98

**62**    Vancouver Province October 17, 1939, p. 22

**63**    Letter from Jean Furse, The Stands, Harwood Street, Vancouver, July 16, 1927

# CHAPTER SEVEN
## AN AFFAIR OF THE HEART

It took seven years from the death of his 'Missus' before Dun-Waters had the desire to remarry. Despite Katie's devotion, his target wasn't her hand. We'll never be certain of their relationship. Katie carefully burned most of her letters, cards and diaries before her death and never spoke of "Dunny" outside the most discreet circle of friends.

We do know that Dun-Waters fell head over heels for a lass from Forres, Scotland, not half his age. A brief diary, hidden amongst her personal photos at least partially explains why.

Margaret Menzies was born April 1, 1895 and lived in Forres until she was 18 when she moved to Edinburgh

The 'crazy man's walk' to the Manor House, so called because Dun-Waters would arbitrarily reassign field hands to weed picking in the gardens. *Photograph courtesy of B.C. Properties Ltd. collection.*

Burnside, originally built for Ronald Pym, was where Katie and Geordie lived until their deaths following Dun-Waters' second marriage. *Picture courtesy O'Keefe Historic Ranch archive.*

"to take up the study of shorthand and typewriting".

She served in various jobs including four years in the typing department of the National Steel Foundry in Leven, before she and her family decided to pull up stakes and move to her brother and his wife who had previously settled at Point Grey in Vancouver. Margaret was 25.

Life with her mother and father, sister Emily and brothers Ian and Joe, was a hard one. For a time she worked as a legal steno for Livingston & O'Dell Barristers, but the firm was not successful and the pay cheques small and often illusive. Monthly it was a struggle to pool their incomes and pay the rent.

When she and her sister Emily were approached to work in a start-up secretarial service, they jumped at the chance. They were to receive $80 a month and 50% share in any profits after expenses. They began their new careers on April 9, 1921 but discovered immediately just how competitive the secretarial service business was in Vancouver at the time.

Many offices had been organized to deal with typing and correspondence for businessmen in the downtown Vancouver core. Emily and Margaret spent most of their time canvassing for assignments and accepted what work they could find often a far less than the going rates.

It took them four years to establish themselves with regular clientel, which included several small law firms and brokers and occasional work for businessmen visiting the Hotel Vancouver.

At 61, on just such a visit to Vancouver for business, Dun-Waters asked the hotel to once again supply 'the bonny lass' who'd typed for him on his last trip. Margaret Menzies was that woman.

This picture, taken before her marriage, shows the age difference between Margaret and her new husband clearly. *Picture courtesy Menzies family collection.*

On that opportunity, Dun-Waters proposed marriage to the 30 year-old. Was he seeking to generate an heir? Was he simply lonely? No written indication remains, but he brought the young woman back to Fintry and gave her a honeymoon on horseback while he hunted and fished!

The Stuarts who had been living with Dun-Waters in the Manor House, moved permanently to Burnside.

The relationship between Katie and Margaret is clouded now, with no one remaining alive who can clarify what the marriage meant to Katie. In his article, "The Dun-Waters of Fintry", David Falconer claimed the marriage was much disapproved of by the Stuarts and that Katie would not speak to the new Mrs. Dun-Waters until just before Dun-Waters' death. But Mrs. Dun-Waters denied that such animosity existed. In fact, when the Falconer article appeared in the 38th Okanagan Historical Society Report, Margaret insisted on a retraction.

In a letter incorrectly written to Kenneth Ellison as a Society representative, she stated:

"May I suggest that if you plan to publish articles similar to that concerning my late husband in your most recent magazine issue that you

To a woman used to earning $80 a week, a honeymoon on horse-back, with her wealthy husband and several ranch hands, might have seemed exotic. *Photograph courtesy of Menzies family collection.*

change the name of the periodical. Anything less "historical" than that collection of malicious, tasteless and irresponsible misstatements would be impossible to imagine.

"I should appreciate your informing your membership that, contrary to the footnote to the article, I was not interviewed by the writer. I was approached, and I told him as I have told others approaching me for the same purpose, that I could not at this date depend on my memory to recall authentic detail about my husband's property.

"May I quote something I have just read which seems to apply precisely to this case:

'An assassin and a slanderer are the same thing. They use different weapons. The assassin uses a gun and the slanderer uses his pen. He uses his pen and destroys the most precious thing a man has - his reputation.'

"When the slandered are no longer alive and cannot speak for themselves the crime is even more heinous." [1]

In the Society's defense, and the defense of Falconer, the President, Victor Wilson, replied but refused to back down.

"Your late husband, Captain Dun-Waters, known far and wide as the Laird of Fintry, was loved and respected by all who knew him. Be-

Katie moved to Burnside permanently with the arrival of the new "mistress". *Photograph courtesy of B.C. Properties Ltd. collection.*

cause he had an unparalleled zest for living no study of him could omit the colour and breadth of his life which has now become legend."[2]

Perhaps Margaret was sensitive at having private matters openly exposed. Certainly no such dislike between Margaret and Katie persisted later in their lives, for in the 1960s Katie was regularly driven into Kelowna for an afternoon visit with Margaret and they even travelled to the U.S. together on at least one occasion.

Still there

Daily, the "master" would stroll to Burnside to have tea with Katie. On occasion he didn't return until the next day. *Photograph courtesy of O'Keefe Historic Ranch archive.*

131

Katie often entertained "Dunny" on their hunting trips by playing the tin whistle. *Photograph courtesy B.C. Properties Ltd. collection*

had to have been some animosity. Dun-Waters regularly crossed the property from the Manor House to Burnside to share tea with Katie and often remained at the house overnight. The correspondence already mentioned between him and Katie also testifies to an abiding relationship between the two.

For more than a decade, Dun-Waters lived with his wife at one end of the property and his life-long friend and companion, Katie, at the other. It didn't seem to inhibit life at Fintry at all, although the "odd" circumstances are recalled as being discussed amongst the Menzies household in Vancouver in hushed tones and "behind closed doors".

Dun-Waters and Margaret enjoyed the pleasures to be had on Okanagan Lake and kept a motor launch for recreation and travel to Vernon and Kelowna. In 1935 however, an accident came close to killing both the 71 year-old and his second wife.

The launch was refitted with a 1934 model Wolseley engine, a motor that used high-octane aviation gasoline. On the day of the accident, Dun-Waters and Margaret had planned on a leisurely boat ride and were

Margaret poses on the looping stone, a stair used by female guests to climb onto their mounts. *Photograph courtesy Menzies family collection.*

Dun-Waters and Margaret pose in Scottish attire a short time before his death. *Photograph courtesy of O'Keefe Historic Ranch archive.*

trying to move the launch from its shed beside the packing house. The engine, however, reluctantly refused to start. Angus Gray heard the Scot's curses and appeared to help. While Margaret waited at the bow with their dogs, Gray cranked the engine.

It appears that fuel had leaked into the bilge of the boat because a spark suddenly ignited the boat and boat house both! Margaret was able to leap to safety onto the dock but both Gray and Dun-Waters were burned in the explosion. Gray made every effort to save the older man by pushing his employer off one side of the boat and then diving into the water on the other. He managed a swimming rescue of a dazed Dun-Waters, dragging him out of the boat house just as the heavy doors collapsed.[3]

Gray suffered severe burns in the incident and for many years afterwards wore Indian-made deer-skin gloves when he worked on the grounds. These gloves form part of the exhibit at the O'Keefe Ranch museum today.

A year after the accident, now 11 years since his second wedding, Dun-Waters decided it was time to make some final changes at Fintry. Without an heir to whom he might pass his estate, Dun-Waters conceived

133

Dun-Waters' launch was outfitted with a polished steel bow constructed to a razor-sharp edge . Sometimes however, as can be witnessed by this image of Dun-Waters with a paddle, technology failed him. *Photograph courtesy of B.C. Properties Ltd. collection.*

a plan for sale. He began to look for a suitable buyer and offered the 2500 acres with its houses, buildings and orchards at sale for $100,000 ($1.2-million adjusted to year of writing). His price seems reasonable enough considering the fact that he estimated an investment in the property of over $500,000 ($6 million adjusted to year of writing).

"If people knew how much I've spent on Fintry — every cent I could get my hands on — I'd be bundled off to a mental hospital," he was quoted as saying.[4] In his offer he retained only Burnside and 20 acres at the mouth of Short's Creek for his home. Using the same type of document he used to sell Culcreuch in Scotland, he described the property in genteel terms in a glossy advertising brochure:

. "Fintry is an ideal property for a keen sportsman seeking a centre for his outdoor activities. It is equally desireable as an estate for the man who is looking for a sound investment, likely to appreciate in value, that will also provide him with a delightful home and a good income. Lastly Fintry could be transformed into a first class hunting and fishing club..."[5]

The 1930s was not the best time in the economic history of Western Canada and no offers resulted from his brochure. Dun-Waters decided instead to turn to an old acquaintance from Cambridge and relinquish his dream of Fintry to younger hands. Retaining Burnside and the mentioned lot, in July of 1938 he donated the property to the Fairbridge Farm Schools Society.

Dun-Waters saw the perfect means to finance the school from the

134

The ill-fated boathouse and Dun-Waters' launch. The women in the picture have not been identified. *Photograph courtesy of O'Keefe Historic Ranch archive.*

production of apples at Fintry, and he threw himself into the plan with his customary gusto. Fintry apples were generally larger than the varieties favoured in Britain. To overcome this and to build a market, he coerced a committee of key men to take the responsibility of selling a few boxes each.

The plan was to 'pluck at the heart strings' to set up a profitable overseas market for the Fairbridge produce and it was well received. In 1939, Dun-Waters planned an organizational trip to England to firm up the market he'd created with some consistent orders, but ill health put a stop to that plan. [6]

Because of his prostate cancer, instead of travelling he had to limit himself to restful hours at Burnside, watching with pleasure as the Fairbridge children trooped into his Manor House turned into dormitory.

"He expressed his pleasure, more than once, at the fact that he had been spared to see the first group of young lads come to the new school institution that he had helped to found on Okanagan Lake." [7]

Despite his ill health, Dun-Waters tried to participate in special events at the school including Sunday picnics and field days. In September 1939, though gravely ill, he travelled to Vernon with the Fairbridge boys to introduce them to the Armstrong Fair in 'true Scot style'. Dun-Waters was known to the regular attendees at the fair as 'The Laird' and he led the pipers into the ring that opening day attired in kilt and tam under the recording eye of National Film Board cameras.

While in Vernon, at a special dinner he organized for the boys in the National Hotel, Dun-Waters marked the occasion with a shiny new silver dollar secretly placed under each boy's dollop of ice cream.

The Fair and other Scottish institutions were often at the receiving end of his generosity and patronage, including the Kildonnan Pipe Band at Vernon which he helped establish as a prominent contibutor in 1937.[8]

Dun-Waters was proud of his heritage and personally designed Christmas and New Year's cards which always had a Scottish touch.

For example, his 1917 New Year's card had a verse entitled, My New Year's Wish which stated:

"Though I'm far awa' frae Scotland,
    And the Land we lo'e sae weel.
Ther's a beat for Auld Country
    In ever pulse I feel." [9]

In the months that followed, Dun-Waters health continued to deteriorate despite schedules of treatment in the Vernon Jubilee Hospital and elsewhere. On one such search for relief in California, he wrote a card to Katie. The card, showing pressed California Sea Moss Dun-Waters identified as 'Flowers of the Sea' and reported:

"I am late in Santa Cruz writing but better late than never! The warm weather has helped my condition. Please excuse pen. I am still advised not to read or write much. The birds singing around the Brae and the wild flowers so pretty. How I wish I could have been in London for the Coronation. I am sorry for our ex-King, poor fellow. I hope you and George keep well. Health is the greatest blessing on earth. Long may our love keep."

Dun-Waters finally gave up on cures. During the noon hour of Monday, October 16, 1939 he quietly passed away.

After a quiet funeral service the following day at Fintry, officiated by Rev. W.W. McPherson of Kelowna, his body was loaded into the back of a truck, covered with a tarp and driven away. In Vancouver, it was cremated.

Dun-Waters death was met with a mix of sadness and public acknowledgment in newspapers around the world. Some not so flattering comments were also received from those who had known him.

E.W. Beatty, President and Chairman of the C.P.R. for example, made light of the passing in a letter to Margaret. Beatty knew Dun-Waters as a key investor in the C.P.R. and he had traveled to the Okanagan at least once in his private railway car to pay a visit to Fintry. In a personal letter sent to Margaret he actually jokes about Dun-Waters death:

"It left me with very mixed emotions, and I really do not know whether to congratulate you or to offer you my sympathy. It was just like him, however, to pass out after he received my cheque, and no doubt cashed it, rather than before.

"Some years ago I read a very interesting book entitled 'Better Dead'. The author is unknown, but perhaps you could get a copy, as a perusal of it would comfort you if indeed you need any.

"I suppose it is foolish to speculate as to where your husband went when he left. Knowing his personal characteristics, I know that, if he had any choice in the matter, he would select the place where living was cheapest, but, wherever he is, I presume the majority of his friends, when their time comes, will select the other place.

"I would be glad to extend to you my sincere sympathy if I thought you needed or wanted it. In all seriousness, however, I may say that I regret your loss as well as the loss of my $50.00."

Fittingly, the *Glasgow Herald* devoted a full column to Dun-Waters' obituary however. Recalling his hunting excursions, the obit led off with a recount of his wanderings, stating incorrectly:"...he spent the later years of his life in England and in Western Canada, and he also had travelled extensively in New Zealand and Australia."

"Despite his far-travelled later career Mr. Dun Waters (sic) retained a great affection for the Fintry countryside, a fact borne out by his adopting the name Fintry for his estate in British Columbia. He ran a sheep farm on the hills at Fintry, and about the late 'nineties created something of a sensation by the high price at which he bought a Blackface ram at Lanark sale from the Glenbuck flock.

"From Fintry he removed to Shropshire. He was attracted there by the sport afforded in fox-hunting, and he became the Master of Foxhounds in South Shropshire. When he retired from that office his friends in the hunt staged a notable ceremony in Shrewsbury Market Square when they presented Mr. Dun Waters (sic), in the spring of 1910, with a George III silver mug.

"When the fruit-growers of the Okanagan Valley, whose 'O.K.' brand of apples are now so well known on the Brtitish market, found prices slumping badly and decided to form a growers' marketing organization Mr. Dun Waters was active in their interests. The Okanagan growers' organization was one of the first producers' marketing enterprises ever attempted. It preceded by several years the large-scale Canadian wheat pool that developed in Western Canada between 1925 and 1929.

"By personal appeal and otherwise Mr. Dun Waters (sic) took up the apple-growers' claims for a better share of the British market. He pleaded that all British clubs and hotels should see that they gave their custom to Empire brands of fruit."

Regarding Dun-Waters passion for Ayrshires, the obituary states:
"In this enterprise he appealed personally and through the columns

of *The Glasgow Herald* to breeders of Ayrshire cattle in this country to help him with gifts in kind and with funds to enable a large group of stock to be exported. "

Most however, the obit writer recalled Dun-Waters' generosity.

"Always a lively and vivacious companion, Mr. Dun Waters (sic) was thoroughly unconventional in his outlook. He was a delightful host, and his sociability was infectious. When he was a member of the board of directors of Messrs George Outram and Co. he acted as host on several occasions to the children of members of the staffs of the *Glasgow Herald* and its associated newspapers. These entertainments took various forms, such as a visit to the Royal Theatre pantomime or a gathering in one of the halls in the city to receive Christmas gifts. On such occasion, Mr. Dun Waters (sic) himself figured with zest among the entertainers of the company, with Harry Lauder songs and other contributions."

*The Evening Standard* hailed him as a great war hero: "In the last war Captain Dun-Waters saw service in Egypt, Italy and France. At his own expense he established a military hospital in Cairo."

Even years later the press were still reminiscing about Dun-Waters. *The Vancouver Daily Province* on Tuesday, May 20, 1947 carried a memory piece:

"One of the most enthusiastic breeders of dairy stock ever to settle in British Columbia was the late Capt. J.C. Dun-Waters of Fintry, B.C.

"Capt. Dun-Waters had a herd of the finest Ayrshires possible in the world. He made a gift at one time to the University of British Columbia of valuable foundation stock consisting of his prize bull and a herd of pure bred cows."

"He saw too it that pictures of British Columbia dairy cattle were published at intervals all over the old country. He had photographs made of dairy animals exhibited at Armstrong Exhibition each year. These were syndicated throughout Britain along with reports of judging of the various classes."

"He shipped many of his cattle to China and the herd of the Hongkong Dairy and Cold Storage company at Hongkong was improved by many high producing cows sent there by Capt. Dun-Waters."

In December 1, 1939, *Maclean's* eulogized Dun-Waters as well. Speaking of his contribution to the Fairbridge Farm School, it stated:

"And for the last year of his life Captain Dun-Waters was happier than he had ever been before. For he felt joy in seeing young Britons, new to this land, learning of its magnificence under the conditions that he had been privileged to develop."

"And he gave it to the Fairbridge interest, so that it might belong to the boys of the future, and thus to the Empire," *Maclean's* continued.

"Just a few weeks before his passing he went to Vernon to see his doctor. In great pain, he confessed that he wanted to brace himself for a little task.

"That evening, in town, he presided at a dinner party for all those fresh-faced boys of the school. Each lad, as he dipped into his ice cream, found a fifty-cent piece (Ed. Note: other reports claim a silver dollar), and each was in turn scrutinized by the kindly eyes of 'the Laird" whose head was high.

"He had sat at lavish dinners the world over, in fact he had given many functions himself for the world's great in many a capital. But this was the last affair over which he was to preside, and he knew it. Yet there was no sadness. His roaring laughter filled the room, and in a little speech he told all the boys that he was proud of them - prouder than they might ever realize."

In 1938, prior to the arrival of the Fairbridge boys, Dun-Waters took steps to preserve his private joy – his hunting trophies. Many, including his prize Kodiak, were donated without charge to the Boy Scout Collection in Kelowna.

According to the Kelowna Museum, the artifacts were collected by George Yochim, Scoutmaster of the 2nd Kelowna Scout Troop, and George Sutherland.

"Originally, they were displayed on the second floor of a barn on David Lloyd-Jones property and then, as the Scout Museum moved premises, to a building south of the Aquatic Centre, in Kelowna.

"The building was moved to the foot of Bernard Avenue and then the collection, in 1958, was moved to the DeMara property, the old Willow Inn guest house, at the foot of Mill Street, when the city purchased the property.

"The Boy Scout collection formed the basis of the collection of the Okanagan Museum and Archives Association when it was incorporated in 1951. When the Kelowna Centennial Museum opened its doors, officially, on June 10, 1967, the OMMA collection was moved into the new building. The Kodiak bear itself was accessioned in 1969; its accession number is KA-69-49-1. It was noted on the accession card that there was wear on the nose at the time so much of the damage was probably done before it came into the present insitution."

While generally accurate, the importance of Dun-Waters' original donations is not properly noted by the museum. Dun-Waters had probably contributed more to the Scout Collection than any other single individual.

The artifacts of all kinds, given to the Scouts for safe-keeping, had been stored in a heatless, tumble-down, condemned two-storey shack until 1945 when the scouts dusted off the 3,000 articles with a goal in mind. In November of 1946, they held a public display of their materials in hopes it would encourage the city and residents in Kelowna to contribute funds for the creation of a museum.

Unfortunately, Dun-Waters prize Kodiak has not weathered well. Over many years of handling, it's snout now worn away by the touching of hundreds of thousands of curious fingers, it languishes in storage at the Kelowna Museum. Wrapped in plastic, it is ratty and unseemly. Hardly a worthy epithet to the donor.

In his will witnessed by Fintry Blacksmith Charles Panton and Manager Angus Gray on May 7, 1938, Dun-Waters left Burnside and its contents to Geordie Stuart and provided for Margaret and Katie with a trust fund. His estate included $225,655 in bonds of 122 companies and 430,149 shares in 30 companies (calculated for the year of writing the bond value would amount to $2.7 million in today's dollar). Geordie and Katie lived in Burnside until their deaths. Geordie in 1963 and Katie in 1968. Margaret, left Fintry for Vancouver and returned a few years later to live in Kelowna with her sisters in a home along the lake near the floating bridge.

Words from the grave can be harsh. Though Dun-Waters didn't legitimize his relationship with Katie through marriage, he showed his affection for her in his last will and testament.

To Margaret he left the sum of $5,000 and bequeathed a Trust to generate an annual income of £1,000. The Trust Fund was to be withdrawn upon her death or remarriage. He also bequeathed her his guns, furniture, household effects and knickknacks, except for the portrait of Alice which was shipped to Charles Orde of Nunnykirk Northumberland.

To Geordie Stuart he left $45,500 and Burnside which was to go to Katie when Geordie died. He also left Katie enough cash for an annuity to generate $3,000 a year (generated by a fund that paid only 3.5%).

To his two Godchildren, Leopold Barclay Paget and his sister, he left $27,750 to share. He gave $5,550 to Grace Beatrice Murray-Menzies of Castle Cottage Doune Scotland and $22,750 to his stock broker.

Margaret, it appears, received the least amount of money in his bequests.

On September 20, 1939, just shortly before his death however, it seems that Dun-Waters may have had a change of heart somewhat. A codicil to his Will changed his bequeath to his godchildren, scaling it down to $18,750.  He also gave Margaret his Graham automobile and allocated $9,000 to her sister Emily and $1,000 to Wong Ying, his manservant.

In the scheme of things, it all must have been a blow to Margaret.  Katie too must have felt the slight.  In a moment of sympathy she wrote to Grace Murray-Menzies about the terms with some evident dismay and indicated that she and Margaret planned a trip together to the Grand Canyon.

Grace replied about the clause that would withdraw Margaret's trust fund income if she remarried by saying: "...she is, as you  say, not very old and did her best by him...strange and ironical that you should be going to see the Grand Canyon with her when you and old Missus used to talk of doing so...I do hope you will be better soon.  So tiresome when you have money and time to knockabout, you aren't fit."[10]

*(Editor's Note: Whether the "Laird" and his "Missus" ever 'left' Fintry is a matter of conjecture.  In the years that followed Dun-Waters' death there were many instances where credible witnesses claimed to have experienced strange happenings in the Manor House, the White House and on the grounds surrounding the dwellings.  Guests in the Manor House reported seeing "tiny lights" floating about in one of the bedrooms at night.  Another claimed to have witnessed what he believed to be a head rolling down the stairway of the White House.  For many years, seekers of the paranormal visited Fintry from around the world, pursuing proof of the hauntings.  None was ever achieved.*

*When the Packing House had been converted into a neighbourhood pub, a shelf of honor was built to display the last remaining bottle of Dun-Waters' private-label scotch.  Invariably each morning would find the bottle turned towards the wall, almost as if the "Laird" wanted to protect his stock from the customers.  It was never determined if the bottle turning was a prolonged prank by either staff or one of the residents.*

*Often, strange noises within the walls of the Manor House were reported.  These however were investigated and attributed to nesting bats that infested the structure at the time.)*

# Chapter Seven Notes

1    Letter from Margaret Dun-Waters, January 11, 1975.
2    Letter from Wilson, January 30, 1975
3    Falconer, D.G. Dun-Waters of Fintry, p. 99
4    Victoria Times, March 25, 1939, p. 6 mag section.
5    *The Fintry Estate*, a glossily illustrated 16-page brochure produced in 1937 to publicize the sale offer
6    Victoria Times, March 25, 1939, p 6 mag section.
7    Vernon News, October 19, 1939, p. 9
8    Vernon News Special *Marching Onward* Edition, October 21, 1937, p. 37
9    Digney, E.F., *Dunwaters Family of Fintry*, p. 5
10   Letter from Grace S. Murray-Menzies, Castle Cottage, Doune, Perthshire, January 18, 1940.

# CHAPTER EIGHT
## A GIFT TO YOUTH

There is no record of how Dun-Waters first came to decide that Kingsley Fairbridge's scheme to train underprivileged and orphaned British children at special farm schools in the Colonies was something to support philanthropically.

The Society had been formed by Oxford Rhodes scholar Kingsley Ogilvie Fairbridge in 1909.

In his memoirs, Fairbridge recounted the day the society was formed.[1]

Fairbridge, just 24 years old himself, had wangled an appearance before 50 members of the Oxford Colonial Club to talk about a plan to find land which could be used in the Colonies to house and train British orphans. He'd already received a positive response about donated land from the Governor of Newfoundland, and needed somehow to raise the funds to put his dream into reality.

"I was on my feet, telling them of the thing that had brought me to Oxford. It was not a simple thing to explain, and it was still more difficult to endow it with life.

"I told them I believed that imperial unity was not a phrase or an artificial thing. Great Britain and Greater Britain are and must be one. Each is in a position to confer untold benefits upon the other; interdependence is therefore their only possible relation.

"The colonies have, above all things, a superfluity of land for the landless men of Britain; Britain has a superfluity of men for the manless land. But whereas the land is good land, the men Britain can spare best are not always good men. The best emigrant farmers have been the aris-

143

tocracy of English yeomen, such as England can ill afford to lose. The colonies should take something that England does not need, if both sides are to profit; something nevertheless that will be an asset to the colony.

"Now there are in England over sixty thousand 'dependent' children - children, orphans or homeless, who are being brought up in institutions, who will be put into small jobs at the age of twelve or fourteen, jobs for which they become too old at eighteen. They have no parents, and no one standing in any such relation to them. What have they before them that can be called a future?

"Here and now, I said, let us found a society to take as many as we can of these children overseas, to train them in our own colonies for colonial farm-life."

He wrote how this plan appeared to him: "It was one of those fiercely hot summer days, when one closes one's eyes against the glare that beats off the road and the iron houses, and as I walked, I ruminated. One sees things that have remained half hidden at the back of one's brain. I saw great Colleges of Agriculture (not work-houses) springing up in every man-hungry corner of the Empire. I saw little children who had no opportunities stretching their legs and minds amid the thousand interests of the farm. I saw unneeded humanity converted to the husbandry of unpeopled areas".

Fairbridge's appeal led to the founding of the "Society for the Furtherance of Child Emigration to the Colonies", afterwards incorporated as the Child Emigration Society (CES). The society raised £2,000 and in 1913 the first "farm school" was opened in on 65 ha (160 acres) at Pinjarra, near Perth, Australia. Another training farm (supported by grants from the British and Australian governments and by private donations) was later established in the state of New South Wales.

It was Fairbridge's dream to create a rural, village-like environment for the children. The girls taken in would receive training in domestic pursuits, and the boys would be trained in manual arts and agriculture. Vocational training was to be supplemented with moral guidance and leavened with recreational pursuits in such a way that the young emigrants would be able to take their places as productive citizens in the host communities.

When war was declared less than a year later in 1914, Fairbridge tried to join the Army, but was turned away because of a medical history of malaria. It gave Fairbridge time to think about the future. The war would leave many more children orphans after all.

Fairbridge wrote to an old Oxford friend, Harry Logan, who by that time had become a Professor of Classics at the fledgling University of

144

British Columbia: "I have long thought that the Child Emigration Society should establish our second farm school in British Columbia. From what I saw there, you have room for tens of thousands of budding farmers. As thanksgiving for our far-flung Empire, I think a good farm school in B.C. would be far more reverent, beautiful and lastingly recognized than some artistic creation that only tends to congest traffic in a main thoroughfare". He'd planted a seed that would bloom years later.

A decade after his death - when the CES was reconstituted as Fairbridge Farm Schools (Inc.) - an appeal was launched to help bring the farm school concept to the dominion. The plight of Britain's unemployed always had the concerned sympathy of Edward, Prince of Wales (the future Duke of Windsor). In 1934, he and Prime Minister Stanley Baldwin campaigned for funds to establish a farm education school in British Columbia. They received $500,000 of which the Prince of Wales donated $5,000. The funds were sufficient to purchase a 445 ha (1,100 acre) site, formerly the estate of F.B. Pemberton, at Cowichan Station, near Duncan, on Vancouver Island.

Not unlike Dun-Waters in financial background, Frederick B. Pemberton who had vast real-estate holdings and financial businesses, named his estate "Pemberlea". It too was a model farm, with fine horses, a registered dairy herd, sheep, and poultry. Unfortunately for Pemberton the stock market crash in 1929 left him practically penniless and unable to maintain it. He sold his last asset, his beloved farm, to the Society.

In 1935, the new facility - officially named The Prince of Wales Fairbridge Farm School, became home to 27 boys and 14 girls, ranging in age from five to thirteen and one-half years. Each group of fourteen lived as a family in a cottage under the guidance of an experienced house mother. They shared all the activities of farm life, and were given the academic schooling required by B.C.'s Ministry of Education until they were sixteen years of age.

For two years after that the boys devoted themselves to learning all types of agriculture, and the girls the arts of domestic science and the chores of a farmer's wife. The Fairbridge staff members looked after the welfare of the children and banked half the earnings of their boys and girls until they came of age at 21 years. Each graduate was then given a nest egg with which to start living independently.

The Fairbridge School was managed like a British residential school. There was an active program of sports - basketball, soccer and boxing (as a Rhodes Scholar, Kingsley Fairbridge had won the Oxford Blue for boxing) during the winter months, and softball, cricket and rugby during the summer. The girls played basketball and went for hikes and treasure hunts.

145

At the Fairbridge School, the children were happy to settle into a secure, well-organized routine. After making their own beds, they took turns doing complete jobs assigned by the cottage mothers on a rotating basis. Two children waxed and polished the dormitory floor while others did household chores. After school came another hour of chores. As the cottages had wood stoves, the boys were busy chopping and stacking wood. The children were work equals - girls did their share of milking, and often came home to meals cooked by the boys. There were always sports activities in the evenings.

Dun-Waters seems to have taken an early interest in the Fairbridge concept. With the creation of the Prince of Wales farm in 1936, Dun-Waters presented the school with a starter herd of Ayrshire. The following year the school purchased another six cows from the Fintry herd, at prices that were predictably favourable.[2]

Kingsley Fairbridge's plan to people the far-flung British possessions with hard-working young Britishers was also recognized in 1936 by Rudyard Kipling. When he died, Kipling provided for his wife and daughter, and then bequeathed the remainder of his estate, valued at $775,000, to be divided among the three Fairbridge schools (a third one had been opened in Australia that year).

That gesture was followed quickly thereafter by Dun-Waters' donation of Fintry on June 27, 1938 for $1, and a period of prosperity for the school seemed assured.

In March, 1939, Governor-General, Lord Tweedsmuir, and his wife Lady Tweedsmuir, who had been a member of the Farm School Society in the London Head Office, visited. The B.C. Government had given Lady Tweedsmuir Sphinx Island in the Strait of Georgia and she in turn donated it to Fairbridge School. In May of that year King George VI and Queen Elizabeth, during their Canadian tour, visited Victoria and to commemorate the Royal tour, an anonymous English M.P. (later identified as Captain Richard Porritt), founded a $23,400 trust fund to aid the Fairbridge schools.

With the Fintry donation, the Society acted quickly to make use of the training potentials. On July 19 three of the senior boys from Duncan were dispatched to the care of Angus Gray. (Geordie took this opportunity to retire from active duty at Fintry). Gray retained the crew at Fintry to ensure that operation continued to generate revenue.[3]

Rather than make the school a residential facility like Duncan, the Society determined Fintry would better serve as a place for 'graduate' training. The older boys from Duncan, were to be sent to Fintry during the summers of their last year or two to 'finish' their training in practical farming on a working concern. They returned to Duncan after the harvest.

In June of the following year, Dun-Waters was overjoyed to greet a group of 28 boys and four girls, all between the ages of 12 and 16 years. The boys had been sent to Fintry to work in the orchards and learn all about spraying, thinning, picking and packing fruit. The girls, who were supervised by two of the school's 'cottage mothers' did the cooking, cleaning and general housekeeping.

Their regime at Fintry was nearly military. Each of the boys was required to invest six hours every day working in the orchard on a schedule that began at 6:30 am.

The change in ownership of Fintry necessarily required some changes to the Manorhouse. For example, Dun-Waters' pride and joy, his trophy room, suddenly became a playroom with ping pong table in the corner and shelves with children's books. The verandah was quickly converted into sleeping quarters with 28 iron cots set in rows.

The 1939 detachment of children returned to Duncan that fall: 15 older children in early September; the rest after the apple harvest.

According to school records, that year of the 11, 081 boxes of apples in the harvest, 5,000 were shipped to Britain. Much of the shipment was earmarked for subscribers to the Fairbridge School which generated considerable interest. Unfortunately, the onset of war meant this clever promotional ploy was not repeatable.

Because of wartime dangers on the Atlantic, no new children were sent to the Canadian school operation. Populations of children dwindled as the older students graduated and entered the work force on Vancouver Island. While the summer schedule of children to Fintry continued through the war, it too gradually slowed to a trickle. In 1940, only 18 boys and two girls were sent to Fintry from June to October. In 1943 that number had shrunk to just seven boys.

By January, 1945 the school had only 100 residents, although there was room for twice that number. And, while British contributions to the Duncan Fairbridge School had been larger than ever in the 1946-1948 period, funds could not be sent to Canada because of restrictions imposed by the British government on exchange of Sterling currency for Dollars.

·      Under the management of Angus Gray, Fintry continued to be productive during the war years and with the end of hostilities, the Society hoped to expand the operation at Fintry Fairbridge. In fact, Sir Charles Hambro, then Chairman of the Council of the Fairbridge Society wrote Gray full of optimism:

"Now that we are allowed to expand once more I hope before long

The first summer that the Fairbridge Farm School took over Fintry, Dun-Waters was happy to see each of the boys attending one of the Aryshires at that year's Armstrong Fair. *Photograph courtesy of O'Keefe Historic Ranch archive.*

that Fintry will become more and more active as a centre for teaching boys the more advanced agricultural methods and a post-graduate school for Old Fairbridgians. In fact I should like to see it the centre of Old Fairbridgians employed on the mainland and a place to which they come for holidays and advice." [4]

But Hambro's optimism was unfounded. Without a flow of capital, the school could not operate. Fintry was to become the first casualty of the crimped finances. The Fintry Fairbridge Training Farm sub-committee chairman P. Walker filed a report to the Board of Governors in 1948 , recounting 10 months of earnest efforts to keep the training farm alive.

In the fall of 1947 an offer of $55,000 was received by the Society for Fintry, but the Board of Governors turned it down. Instead they attempted to open negotiations with the Canadian Pacific Railway "whereby Fintry would become available for Displaced Persons." Seven months of correspondence and discussion however proved fruitless and on October 13 the Yorkshire and Pacific Securities Ltd. negotiated the sale of the property to Richard T. Perry and William C. Prater of Yakima, Washington for $65,000. After commissions and taxes, the Society expected to pocket $60,000 from Dun-Waters' gift. [6]

Included in the sale was the Fintry Aryshire herd of 31 cattle with an estimated value of $4,525. [7]

148

Over the 10 year period that Fintry was owned by the Society, the London office had supplied $93,946.11 for operating and maintenance purposes. This was partially recouped by way of apples ($14,103.92) which were shipped from Fintry to London and sold by the London office in 1939. Even so, the Society lost nearly $20,000 by accepting Dun-Waters' gift.

Total losses at Fintry from 1938-1947 were recorded as $38,992.76 with losses in 1948 about $4,000 more.

Inspite of the financial difficulties, the report paid tribute to Angus Gray.

"As this is probably the last report that will be made on Fintry, it seems appropriate to set forth a tribute to the skill, ability and efficiency of Mr. Angus Gray who was our superintendent. He stayed with us the whole time and took a great weight off the shoulders of this Committee."

The financial death of the Society continued until August, 1949 when the Society decided to close all their schools. The Society decided to retain the Fairbridge property on Vancouver Island until the current class graduated. Hearing of the problems, the Canadian Pacific Railway Company proposed to lease the Vancouver Island estate and bring selected British farm families there, under its Department of Immigration and Colonization. These settlers would have to have the minimum transferable funds, and would agree to farm the Fairbridge property for three years.

But the continuing financing problems in Britain prevented the parent Fairbridge Society from sending their wards to Canada, and from re-opening a Farm School on the Vancouver Island estate. In March, 1950, it was rented by the B.C. dairy firm, Stevenson and McBryde, from the C.P.R. The dairy inherited from the capable veteran administrators of the Fairbridge School: 70 head of purebred Ayrshire cattle in the herd started by Dun-Waters' donation.

For Fintry, the sale of the estate to American interests heralded a period of neglect. The property passed through several sets of hands, each less interested than the last. When a series of unusually cold winters killed a large number of the Fintry fruit trees, a tourist camp was established on the delta.

Strangely, it was that little unkempt tourist campground that led to a new halcyon period for Fintry.

149

# Chapter Eight Notes

1    Fairbridge, K., *The Story of Kingsley Fairbridge*, Oxford Uni
     versity Press, 1927, pp 173-174
2    Fairbridge Farm Schools, Annual Reports 1934, p 19; 1936,
     pg 28 ; 1937 p. 32
3    Vernon News, July 14, 1938, p 1; Vancouver News Herald,
     July 21, 1938, p. 7
4     Letter from Sir Charles Hambro to Angus Gray dated 1945,
     Vernon Museum Archives
5    Fintry Fairbridge Training Farm Report for 1948
6    Vancouver Province, October 29, 1948, p. 1; and a letter from
     Logan Mayhew, Chairman of    the B.C. Board of Governors
     of Fairbridge, to Mr. And Mrs. Angus Gray, October 20, 1948,
     in Vernon Museum Archives.
7     Letter from Angus Gray to Mr. Newton of the B.C. Ayrshire
     Breeders' Assn. July 18, 1949, in Vernon Museum Archives

# CHAPTER NINE
## FABULOUS FINTRY - BY MAIL

By 1958, owned by Mortenson and Kazor of Seattle, Fintry was a mess. Hardly a glimmer of it's former glory, the property was occupied only by Katie and her brother Geordie who continued to live as Fintry's only residents in their beloved Burnside.

But Fintry had not been forgotten by men with vision.

With Kelowna's Tom Capozzi as a catalyst, several of them were getting together in Vancouver watering holes to talk about the potentials of development in the Okanagan. One, a man named Stan James, eagerly promoted Terrace Mountain behind Fintry as a prospective ski resort. While the men who listened to James had no interest in ski resorts, the prospects of land development at Fintry intrigued them. That December with James' eloquent descriptions in mind, three interested parties decided to see for themselves.

Sidney A. McDonald was a stout, two-fisted drinking oilman from Calgary and a good friend of Cap and Tom Capozzi. He was familiar with the Okanagan's potential having visited the valley on several occasions. McDonald had been in the oil business for the ten years previous, first as a drilling contractor and then as a producer. When he retired he was vice-president of Albermont Petroleums Ltd. which amalgamated with Western Decalta Petroleum Limited. Prior to that, he had been in the hotel business and aviation. He was an entrepreneur at heart and a 'demon for the deal'.

With him was Bert Plaxton, a politically-connected lawyer who had served in the Ministry of Defence under W.L. Mackenzie-King and earned himself the nickname of the "Merchant of Death" because his war work included some responsibility for the manufacture of Sten guns.

Arthur Bailey, step-son to one of Vancouver's wealthiest financiers also joined them.

A business success in his own right, Arthur Bailey was a 30 year-old land developer who had cut his teeth creating the lucrative Windsor Park development in the Seymour Mountain area of North Vancouver. He had previously lived in California and was eager to employ the techniques he saw working there, for the residential development successes in Canada. For example, Bailey was the first developer to secure approvals to build high-rise residential buildings on the West Vancouver waterfront. His projects included the Capilano Highlands development among others. Bailey also co-published a national tourism magazine called 'Canada in Colour' with West Vancouver photographer, Bill Gibbons and was the first to introduce the closed-circuit television system promoting local tourist attractions now so familiar to visitors in Vancouver hotels. Bailey and McDonald had something else in common too. Their mutual friendships with the Capozzi family.

The men arrived at Fintry late one afternoon that December, guided to the property by John McAllister, a former employee of McDonald's who had moved to Kelowna. Fintry was draped in a thick blanket of snow the day they arrived, silent and deserted. McAllister, who needed to return to town immediately for his wedding, advised the men not to drive their car back to Kelowna on the Westside Road after dark.

Fintry was an expanse of emptiness, marked by animal tracks and little else. The men were enthralled by the immense size of the property. It was a beautiful spot and what amazed them most was that no one had, it appeared, realized that the delta was prime for development.

They examined the Manor House, a beautiful stone edifice with a sweeping verandah that overlooked extensive grounds. There seemed to have been gardens, they surmised. Was that an old tennis court? They all agreed that someone had obviously put a lot of care into the place in the past, and had been given a sketchy tale about a wealthy old Scot who had lived on the property and given it away to a British school before he died. The school had quickly fallen on hard times he told them, and sold the property to some Americans. The Americans had let it disintegrate.

They wandered the property and noted that, unlike the barns and bunkhouses they'd seen, the 'mansion' had been left relatively unmolested by vandals. Except for malicious window breaking, it remained in good shape.

By the time they had finished their walking tour of the property it was late afternoon and the sun had begun to set. The men were cold and wet. The absolute last thing they wanted to do, they all agreed, was drive that road back to Kelowna at night. Besides, there were too many ideas being shared, too many things to consider. Briefly discussing whether it was legal and deciding it was either freeze to death outside or find shelter inside, Sid put a shoulder to a door on the abandoned house and led his companions into history. To their amazement, the house still contained some furniture including a few roughly built tables. Hastily, because by now they were shivering in the sub-zero weather, the men broke one down into kindling and lit themselves a fire in one of the house's many fireplaces.

Sid, relaxing in the glow of the flames, magically exposed the ever-present bottle of scotch he had tucked in his pocket. He urged his friends to relax.

In his opinion, Fintry would be an ideal place to retire.

"We're going to be here all night anyway. What we need to do before we leave is draft a purchase agreement," he told them. "We'll figure out how we're going to sell it afterwards."

With the bottle passed back and forth and Plaxton scribbling in long-hand, McDonald worked through versions of purchase agreements, toyed with various ideas on how to develop the property and divided up future tasks. It took them most of the night to complete their lists, but by the time the sun came up Sid had agreed to find the money. Art agreed to undertake the development of the property if it ever reached that point.

On their return to Vancouver McDonald made fast work of negotiating the purchase of the Short's Creek delta land from Mortenson & Kazor in Seattle and of the High Farm pasture land from the Roy family in Yakima. The offers were fair and both owners, not particularly interested in the land anyway, gladly sold.

McDonald quickly formed two companies. One he called Fintry Estates Ltd. and the other Fintry Estates Utilities Ltd. He gathered a small coterie of friends and former business associates as advisors, some of whom agreed to act as investors or directors. They included H. F. Waste, an executive with the Bechtel Corp. in San Francisco, Stan James and Art Bailey.

With his background in the cash intensive oil business, McDonald was conscious of the need to have skilled promoters involved if he wanted to see Fintry Estates Ltd. happen as he dreamed. Stan James said he knew just the man for the job, a gambling crony of his named Barney Auld.

Auld had proven skill 'spinning gold from straw', though his friend had allegedly been involved with other businessmen who he vaguely recollected may have been charged with mail fraud. All that aside, James told McDonald, Auld would be an ideal fellow to help launch McDonald's dream for a retirement development. He was right, but as it turned out, Auld also provided the spark that would soon vault McDonald into the national newspaper headlines and force new legislation on land speculation to be created in the B.C. Legislature.

While gregarious and skilled as a promoter, Auld was also a shady type with a background some might find questionable. Hailing from New York, he dressed and acted like he'd been pulled from the pages of a Damon Runyon novel. He regularly carried a hand-gun, was rumored to be living with a notorious Vancouver madam and cultivated friendships with the rich and famous of the day, including movie-star Errol Flynn.

Auld was happy to get involved in the Fintry project. Perhaps it was because he saw it as a way to finally use his skills in a legitimate enterprise, Auld fit easily into the group of entrepreneurs. He liked

Barney Auld. *Photo courtesy B.C. Properties Ltd. collection*

McDonald's gregarious style. Auld introduced McDonald and Bailey to some of his many 'contacts', including Errol Flynn. On several occasions, between joining 'the team' and the actor's heart attack and death that October, Sid hosted them all at long, raucous evenings of dining and dancing in The Cave, Vancouver's most popular nightclub at the time. Bailey now recalls Flynn always dressed casually in a navy blue sports jacket and running shoes, gesticulating with his long cigar holder while he talked about starlets. He remembers McDonald happily matching the alcoholic actor, drink for stiff drink all night long, and how neither showed signs of impairment despite the copious quantities. With

Auld's flamboyant image, and those sorts of connections, it's no wonder McDonald agreed to the promoter's idea about how to sell Fintry.

'The retirement idea is good. It's going over big in the States,' Auld counselled. 'I think you should sell it like they've been flogging land in Florida! Make it easy to buy! A tenner down and a ten-spot a month but no title until it's paid off."

Despite his own normally easy-going inclination to do deals with a handshake, McDonald was careful about following Auld's advice. The legalities of a Florida-style land sale made him uneasy. He consulted his lawyer Fred Russell. Auld's entire plan was reviewed, including every piece of promotion that Auld was recommending. His solicitors confirmed that everything suggested was entirely legal.

In early 1959 McDonald ordered Peter Amcotts, an internationally recognized engineer, to complete a perimeter survey of the property and stake lots, inspite of several feet of snow and unseasonably cold weather.

As soon as possible, Auld wanted to act. He wanted to make sure he could entice farming prospects with visions of sandy beaches and warm weather that winter ' while they're staring out their windows at a blizzard!' Auld's scheme was to devise a slick newspaper ad campaign that promoted minimum 7,500 sq. ft. lots for an affordable $795. McDonald liked the idea. Even at that price, a sellout would generate $3,975,000 from lot sales!

After Auld completed his advertising campaign, he suggested that Fintry Estates Ltd. 'arms-length' themselves from the marketing by hiring a separate group to handle the sales effort. McDonald agreed with Auld and put Stan James in charge.

Auld's full-page ads were booked in newspapers across the country and the U.S., in several languages, as soon as the property survey was received by Fintry Estates Ltd.

"$10 secures your homesite in the sunny Okanagan," the newspaper ad began. "To live in a home of your own design, beside the sparkling blue waters of a lake famed the world over for its colorful water sports - this is a prospect so inviting most Canadians will scarcely have dared entertain it. Yet today, you can own a homesite in this location for less than the price of a pack of cigarettes a day!"[1]

To match the enticing image, Auld had carefully set up photos of a young family in swim suits, with their picnic basket and beach umbrella, ready to enjoy their property. He added pictures of a fishing boat, complete with a man holding up what might easily be guessed as a 20 lb. trout, and a mirror-quiet lake in the background. He described Fintry in glowing terms, like a country club, making liberal use of the facilities that Dun-Waters had incorporated at the property. "It already has a large steamer dock, tennis courts, golf driving range, paddocks, boats and many other improvements. A marina, Olympic-sized community swimming pool, etc. are soon to be added. Water and electricity are included."

The ad highlighted an aerial photograph of the delta and continued by saying: "Only the best sections are being utilized for home-sites; the remainder has been left in parkland, which includes bridle paths, lakes stocked with fish and a spectacular 100 foot waterfall."[2]

To overcome fears of a real-estate con, Auld carefully inserted an assurance that everyone who decided to make a purchase was being offered a choice homesite and that every purchase came with a 30-day money back guarantee. To prompt fast decisions, he added that the sales were limited to only three lots per person.

"On your first visit to your property you can, without obligation, exchange your lot for any other available home-site of equal value," the promotion claimed. Of course Auld didn't expect many buyers to make the trip from the windy corners of Saskatchewan to Fintry just to check on a $10 investment.

Prairie farmers, frost-bitten and tired of the cold weather, ate it all up like candy.

The sales material touted a long range plan for a community of 16,000 people at Fintry, on 4,500 to 5,000 lots within ten years and by the way their prospects responded it could very well have happened. The news media described the scheme a marvel. Even local politicians got involved extolling the virtues of the idea.

"I feel that it is certainly a marvellous asset, not only to Fintry but to both Vernon and Kelowna," pealed Vernon Mayor Frank Becker[3]

"We believe the area has tremendous recreational possibilities," echoed 38 year-old Stan James. He told the press that "we feel many of our sales will be to people who want to have a place for their retirement or who want a place for a summer home or recreation spot."

Within the first week of offering their $10-down-$10 per month plan, the company recorded more than 1,000 lot sales.[4] James claimed the company "had to triple office staff to keep up with the mail demand." Daily, Jamesw was opening envelopes in the handfuls, withdrawing $10 cheques and allocating spots on a first-come basis by sticking pins into the lot survey.

"They sold several hundred lots in the first 14 days," recalls Bailey, who was watching the goings-on from the sidelines, waiting for his opportunity to be called on to develop the property. "The post office had to send a special truck with the mail. They dumped it at the Howe Street office for sorting. It was just an unbelieveable response!"

What the buyers didn't know of course was the location of their lot. As it turned out, Fintry Estates Ltd. had decided to sell the 'upper benches' first. None of the lots allocated initially were even on the delta. All the sales made were from the Westside Road west.

"It was an alligator. The plan of the properties must have been 15 feet long and as a letter would come in with a $10 bill a little pin would go on this monstrous map," says Bailey. In all cases, the first wave of purchases were allocated land where neither roads, water or sewer were yet built.

When, within weeks, the number of lot sales had jumped to 3,000, the Fintry Estates Ltd. land offer began to draw the attention of consumer watchdogs and the government. Fintry was among several land sale promotions underway in the province and Attorney General Robert Bonner voiced public concern that changes were necessary in the Real Estate Act to safeguard against fraudulent land speculation.

As part of this new interest by consumer organizations, the Vancouver Better Business Bureau made an announcement to the press. They denied that the BBB had given approval to the Fintry developers to use their organization's name in any advertising.

Stan James. *Photo courtesy B.C. Properties Ltd. collection*

McDonald had sent Stan James to the BBB to get their seal of approval, but Bailey recalls that James "was pretty full of himself by then and thought he could walk on water". James arrived for his appointment just as McDonald had directed, but when he was kept waiting in the foyer for 20 minutes, he left in a huff without actually meeting the BBB executive. James neglected to tell McDonald what he had done. When McDonald saw the BBB's blessings in the promotion he thought it was with that organization's permission. It wasn't.

James' ill-advised action made McDonald furious, but worse that expletives shouted in the offices of Fintry Estates Ltd. what James had done started a domino-effect of criticism for the Fintry development's sales activity.

W.L. Templeton, general manager for the Bureau, told the press that salesmen for the Fintry scheme were using the Bureau's name without permission. That obviously made Templeton suspicious of the developer's intent. Templeton told the media that Lakeshore Land and Title Co. was handling the sales for Fintry Estates Ltd. and he identified Lakeshore's principals as Barney Auld, Stanley James and Leo Carlin, of Toronto.

While most of the media didn't bother to investigate too deeply into the backgrounds of the salesman, the Vancouver Sun was more diligent. Reporter Alex Young suggested that the public should be suspicious of a land sale that seemed too good to be true. He turned to the Attorney General for detailed comment and Bonner said that he was in fact drafting a new Real Estate Act because he had similar concerns.

The new act Bonner had in mind would require full and factual disclosure to prospective buyers of details of all promotions; require the registration of subdivision plans for approval by the government's land registry branch and require the licensing of development agents by the Superintendent of Insurance.

The new act was to protect consumers from illegal sales tactics, but the Fintry Estates Ltd. plan was entirely legal according to the laws then existing because each of the proposed lots was a half-acre. Unstaked land could be sold. Land without water supply could be sold. Agents did not need to be specially licensed. All that was legally required for the sale was road access. However, Bonner mistakenly lumped Fintry Estates with questionable development schemes then receiving press that included Eagles Nest Estates Ltd. in West Vancouver, Mount View Housing Ltd. in Ladner and Tsawassen Property Ltd. in Ladner.

Bonner said he wanted to see salesmen licensed as real estate agents. He wanted to have a percentage of revenue from each sale set aside to make service improvements to the properties being sold. That made sense. As mentioned, had the buyers whose lots were assigned on the High Farm plan bothered to pay a visit to Fintry, they would have quickly learned that water and sewer were still a long way off in the development plans.

Inevitably, when the questions began to surface in Vancouver and Victoria, it wasn't long before the media began to ponder them on the Prairies.

"Some buyers from Calgary have driven up to the area and report the property is practically impossible to find and appears to be in a very primitive state. It is entirely undeveloped," one newspaper reported.[5]

By the middle of April the questions being asked forced Sid McDonald to reply to accusations of possible fraud by the Better Business Bureau in his old stomping grounds of Calgary. Sid drafted a six-page telegram.[6]

"It must be remembered that this is not a get-in and get-out situation," he advised. "But rather a long-term project that will not see its fullest development until a few years hence."

"This is a multi-million dollar situation when carried through to its ultimate conclusion," he wrote, "and we are not planning to make any rash and hurried applications in regard to our master planning for the area." Sid had a detailed master plan but failed to send it with his telegram.

Though Sid assured everyone that a master plan was in place, as infact it was, keeping it secret didn't wash with the Better Business Bureau in Calgary. Allan Rose, then the manager there, reviewed the telegram and because he had no other proof of a master plan, told the newspaper, "it still doesn't alter the situation in my mind one bit. I went through the contract again and there isn't one thing in it that commits them to anything."

Rose was right. There wasn't. The contracts were simple agreements that didn't turn over title to the purchased property until the final payment and didn't spell out any obligations by the developer.

By the end of April, the media had formed into a pack of wolves on the hunt. The Vancouver Sun led the charge at Fintry Estates by sending a reporter to the Okanagan to see for himself.

The newspaper reminded the public of warnings from the Vancouver Real Estate Board that buyers should be 'wary of certain types of land selling projects'. Fintry, the reporter wrote, had been priced at $200,000 'a few years ago' and with the subdivision of the property could be worth 'at least $2.5 million', hinting delicately at ulterior motives of greed by the developers.

"A Vancouver Sun reporter who inspected the property last week found that most of the lots being sold at present are about 1,000 feet above Okanagan Lake in a valley," the article said.[7]

"He found that a beautiful, flat point of land jutting into the lake that features prominently in the brochures and advertisements issued by the sales company is not for sale as lots."

The newspaper report was enough to not only cause panic among prospective buyers but some fast footwork in Victoria. By May, Tom Cantell, Superintendent of Real Estate, announced he was drafting new regulations that "will provide for licensing of land speculation companies as well as some form of inspection" similar to measures in the United States.[8]

Interest by Victoria also prompted the local Kelowna City Council to request an explanation of McDonald's plans, but rather than appear before Council, Sid drafted another of his carefully considered letters.

"Rumour and misinformation about our project have combined to paint a wrong and harmful picture," he wrote.[9] "We plan to set before you all the facts on Fintry Estates Ltd. so you and your group may see for yourselves that we have embarked on not only a sober and lawful venture, but one that will bring new life, trade and quickening interest to the Okanagan." Further, he told the Council that money required for development was being held in escrow at the Bank of Montreal, Hastings & Carrall Branch in Vancouver. This, Sid must have felt, would be enough proof of the sincerity the company had for the development, but it still wasn't enough for the scandal hungry media.

Just four days after his written response to the Kelowna Council, McDonald found himself forced to deny rumors that Fintry Estates Ltd.

was being investigated by the government.

"At no time have the officers of the company been approached either by letter or by members of any investigative branch of the government," he told the press.[10]

McDonald promised that "a great portion of the area bordering the lake is being reserved for all lot owners."

"This property, continuous (sic) to the lake, will never be sold to individual lot owners, but set aside as a source of pleasure for all."

When the media could uncover no proof of legal wrong-doing, it seems they turned instead to ridicule. One article on the Prairies warning of scams perpetrated on the honest farmer compared Fintry to a man selling grass seed with claims it would grow eight feet tall. [11]

"Also during the past year, many Edmontonians began at $10 down and $10 a month to buy property for retirement in the Okanagan. One buyer who drove out to see his property never was able to find it. He found he would have to cut his way in through the bush. The land had not been surveyed and, for all he knew, his plot might have been on a perpendicular slope of mountain."

The hubbub however died down until the Penticton Herald again asked about the development's legality a few month's later.

"A query to the provincial government brought the reply that Fintry Estates Ltd. selling land on Okanagan Lake north of Kelowna, has been reorganized.

"The company has dissociated itself from the promitional (sic) element which aroused criticism this spring, said the government letter."[12] The restructuring the government referred to included the hiring of R.M. Randall as the General Manager and director of the development plan.

Because of the regulatory changes pending, Fintry Estates Ltd. had earlier put a halt to their advertising. McDonald low on funds anyway and planning to get married, borrowed cash from Randall to begin providing amenities at Fintry.

In Kelowna, news of that investment and the plan for a 'tent-camp' at Fintry, sold in a public relations effort by Randall, turned around the same City Council that had expressed concerns about Fintry just five months earlier.

"Mayor R.F. Parkinson and the Kelowna Board of Trade have gone on record as supporting the "new" Fintry Estates," it was reported.[13]

Randall was quoted as saying that a trust deed had been registered for 1,170 people and "of the total, 600 people are paying now" indicating to the world that buyers had not lost faith. His numbers, unfortunately, were inaccurate. In actual fact, only 300 or so of the contracts were still in good standing.[14]

"In four or five years, Fintry will be the most popular resort area in the Okanagan," Randall predicted.

The steps in the new plan for development interested people because they were simple. The development was now to begin with a "tent camp" to be built that summer. By the following summer he predicted that a 9-hole golf course would be built at Fintry. Modest classified advertising for the tent camp was placed in newspapers across the Prairies and in the Pacific Northwest. But the problems for the Fintry Estates Ltd. consortium were far from over.

However, with finances for Fintry Estates Ltd. apparently in order, McDonald married and departed on his honeymoon, leaving Randall, his manager, with explicit instructions about how the money he'd borrowed was to be used at the development. In the weeks that followed however, instead of abiding to McDonald's instructions, Randall limited his spending at Fintry to the construction of a wash house (the shower house that now stands in the Park) and a boat launch. The rest, it was alleged, was in another development north of Fintry.

On his return, McDonald discovered that Randall had ignored his instructions. The unauthorized spending and the legal wrangling that inevitably followed because of it left Fintry Estates Ltd. crippled financially. On July 11, 1961 creditors were notified that bankruptcy proceedings were underway for Fintry Estates Ltd..

"At that time there were still 300 people paying $10 a month," out of the 5,000 lots that had been originally sold, says Bailey

Despite what to all others might have seemed a pointless and ill-concieved notion, Bailey still retained his fervent hope that Fintry could again be lifted back to its former glory. He convinced the directors of B.C. Properties Ltd., they should make an attempt to pick up the pieces at Fintry.

"As the Managing Director of B.C. Properties Ltd., I had the company comptroller, Ernst Kaiser, investigating our next land investment. We had him looking at Coal Island near Victoria, and at Fintry. It was decided that Fintry was the best investment due to its size, the fact that we could expect less government red tape for development in the Okanagan and the fact that I had what amounted to inside information on the project."

There are eerie echos of similarity between the early life of Dun-Waters and Bailey. To inherit his fortune, Dun-Waters had been required to change his name. When Arthur Bailey's mother married Ronald Graham after divorcing Art's father some years ealier, Art was only 11 years-old. Unlike Dun-Waters however, Art showed signs of a stubborn will and independent spirit regarding his heritage. He refused to give up his heritage for an inheritance as Dun-Waters had done, hyphenated or otherwise. Afforded the opportunity to drop the Bailey name and become a Graham, thereby becoming a full heir to F. Ronald Graham's wealth upon his death, Art had refused.

That decision came back to haunt him however in F. Ronald Graham's will. Because of his decision decades before, Arthur had no 'inheritance windfall' of his own to purchase Fintry. Although he had a successful development history, it was all accomplished within the B.C. Properties Ltd. corporate shell as the Managing Director. He continued to see the Dun-Waters estate as an ideal resort destination, as a development that could be similar to areas like Arrowhead Lake in California and Lake Tahoe in Nevada, but acquisition of Fintry lands would have to be accomplished through B.C. Properties or not at all.

The company assigned its lawyer, Robert Ross (who had married Arthur's step-sister) to negotiate an agreement with Attorney General Robert Bonner. Ross, working directly with Bonner, successfully crafted guidelines for a B.C. Properties Ltd. bid to the bankruptcy trustees. It was a plan that would ensure all the people who had purchased lots at Fintry would receive property if Fintry was purchased by the company.

The '$10 down' purchasers in good standing were required to continue to pay for their lots if they were to benefit from the deal, but it was also agreed that none of the money being received from them would end up moving to B.C. Properties Ltd. Rather, it went to the creditors of the old bankrupt companies.

With that arrangement crafted by Robert Ross, and blessed by Robert Bonner, B.C. Properties bid $215,000 cash for Fintry and joined the ranks of 20 others[16] who had submitted purchase offers to the trustees for Fintry Estates Ltd., including cowboy singer Gene Autry.[17]

On June 15, 1963, bankruptcy trustee Ian H. Bell accepted B.C. Properties' offer expressly because it meant that "$10 down" landowners still in place on the books could keep their land.

Bailey was overjoyed. He had agreed with the directors of B.C. Properties Ltd. that if the company's bid was successful, he would fund B.C. Properties Ltd.'s operating costs. He had been developing a number of lots in North Vancouver on his own. To come up with his share, he discounted all of those lots and sold them.

Art felt he had reached for the brass ring and miraculously caught it!

Not everyone met the news with a smile of relief. On June 16, what could be considered a prophetic letter predicting a sad future for the Graham/Bailey era at Fintry, was mailed to Mrs. Graham. Bearing insufficient postage and addressed only to "Mrs. F. Ronald Graham, Widow of late financier" it purported to be a warning from a sheep herder.

"Think hard - and - be sure you are not parting with the money. That you may even take your own life by causing too many regrets of having parted with it - later on. I am sure many people made all kinds of money on land dealings since the last war - But for each that makes some-one loses - so, if you have read my scribble may God grant you the time to also Think and Back Out of this deal if you are not prepared to lose - and lose heavy."[18]

Art and Helen ignored the naysayers.

A renewed life for Fintry was about to begin.  Or was it?

# Chapter Nine Notes

1    Direct Mail lure piece developed by Fintry Estates Ltd.
2    ibid
3    Vancouver Province, March 16, 1959
4    Moose Jaw Times-Herald March 28, 1959
5    Calgary Herald, April 9, 1959
6    Calgary herald Satuday April 11, 1959
7    Vancouver Sun April 30, 1959
8    Vancouver Sun May 1, 1959
9    Kelowna Capital News July 1, 1959
10   Kelowna Courier July 4, 1959
11   Edmonton Journal Jan 21, 1960
12   Penticton Herald August 4, 1959
13   Daily Courier Jan 30 1960
14   Vernon Daily News February 4, 1960
15   Vancouver Sun, July 17, 1963; Vancouver Province July 18, 1963
16   Calgary Herald, June 15, 1963
17   Vancouver Province, June 28, 1963
18   Letter June 16, 1963 in Arthur Bailey archive materials

# CHAPTER TEN
## ARISTROCRATIC COINCIDENCES

It's a fitting and curious coincidence following "The Laird" and the other actual aristrocratic previous owners of the Fintry property, that the delta should be rescued from obscurity by another man of title. Arthur Bailey carries the appellation of Baron d'Avray and Chevalier de St. Louis with a quiet and unpretentious attitude almost bordering on disregard. Nonetheless the real aristocratic cognomen and the story of how his family acquired the hereditary title is an interesting sidebar to the Fintry story.

In the late 1700s, Joseph Head Marshall, a newly trained doctor, served time with Dr. Edward Jenner. It was during the period when smallpox was the frightening scourge of both the rich and poor. During the 17th and 18th Centuries smallpox was the most serious infectious disease in the West and accounted for a substantial proportion of deaths, especially among town dwellers. The mortality rate varied regionally, with 10% in Europe.

Various doctors had been practising a form of vaccination promoted in China, charging exhorbitant fees to insert live virus from smallpox victims into cuts made on the arms of healthy individuals. Needless to say the success rate of protection to the disease by their methodology was low to nil. A Dorset farmer, in fear of a smallpox epidemic and unable to afford the expensive 'cure', performed the inoculation process himself. Using a knitting needle he inoculated his wife Elizabeth Jesty and two children using pus from a sore on a cow's udder. His family escaped the 'pox'.

Whether Jenner acted on information about Jesty's success or not is unclear to history, but in 1796 he claimed success against smallpox

165

with vaccination. Despite the confidence of 100 prominent London physcians in Jenner's research, the medical fraternity as a whole was not as supportive. Jenner needed a means to prove the efficacy of his cure and thereby 'own' it. He devised a clever public relations ploy to bring his cure to the attention of the world.

As smallpox was devasting the British troops fighting in the Napoleonic wars, he convinced the Admiralty to allow him to inoculate. When the Admiralty agreed, Jenner dispatched Marshall and another medical assistant named Walker who volunteered their services, to tour British naval vessels at war in the Mediterranean and inoculate the soldiers.

Marshall joined the fleet in October 1802, sailing aboard the HMS Foudroyant to Gibraltar. With the blessing of Lord Keith, he inoculated the men aboard the naval vessels there within days of his arrival and eradicated smallpox on the vessels in a matter of days.[1]

For his services, Marshall was paid £50 by the Admiralty and another £50 by the War Office. The payments barely covered 25 per cent of his expenses, but it didn't deter Marshall from continuing his mission on his own bankroll. He travelled to Sicily when he learned a rampant smallpox epidemic had claimed the lives of 8,000.

With letters of introduction, Marshall was given audience by Ferdinand IV, where he explained the process. Ferdinand, an odious King if ever there was one, ordered a child in Naples be selected at random and inoculated and then exposed to smallpox, not once but twice. When Marshall did as he was told and the child escaped the disease, Ferdinand had himself, Queen Carolina and their children inoculated and then invited all the citizens of Naples to do the same. In a matter of weeks, Marshall had personally inoculated the city, effectively saving the entire population from the disease. Ferdinand was so pleased he had a portrait of the doctor painted depicting Marshall as one of the apostles (the portrait eventually found its way into the galleries of the Vatican).

Marshall continued his tour, visiting Arabia and inoculating everyone he came into contact with. Eventually, out of money and without a supply of vaccine, he returned to England where detractors accused him of all manner of deceit and usury regarding his mission of vaccinations. So loud and vociferous was the criticism, a House of Commons committee was struck to review his tour. It was learned in those hearings that Marshall had personally vaccinated more than 10,000 people.

The editor of Public Character, a rather unique London publication of the time, remarked at the time of the hearing: "On the occasion (of Dr. Marshall's tour) the vast advantage of Dr. Jenner's discovery was conspicuous; and when we recollect how long victory remained doubtful between the two contending armies in the east, it is not unwarranted to suppose that vaccine inoculation had some share in turning the scale and deciding the fortunes of war."[2]

The Parliamentary committee decided to believe Marshall and awarded Jenner £20,000 to open a vaccination clinic in London. Marshall however, was left substantially unrewarded and in disgust over his treatment he moved to France. There, over time, he befriended the Marquis d'Osmond. It was that friendship, and not his herculean vaccination tour, that eventually led to his title.

In January 1815, from conversations with d'Osmond, Marshall learned that Napoleon was intending to leave Elba with his bodyguards and give his personal support to the Bonapartists.

With this secret knowledge, Marshall approached King Louis XVIII, but the King refused to act on the rumour. On February 26, Napoleon departed Elba.

"During the Hundred Days," Marshall later wrote, "I continued to live in Paris, at the great peril of my life. I transmitted twice a week to His Majesty, a report on all the important events that came to my knowledge by way of my intimacy with the Duke of Otrante, with whom I used to spend a part of my day."[3]

In gratitude for this act of espionage, Louis bestowed a pension of 4,000 frances per month on Marshall and the good doctor became a critical intermediary between the British monarchy and King Joachim (Murat) of Naples. Because of these high level connections, Marshall was called upon to help broker a peace treaty between one or more of the Allied Powers and Murat. On one occasion, Marshall applied the same dedication he had for the vaccination tour in the peace process, travelling on horseback the 1,200 miles from Naples to England with secret papers in just 27 days.

"It is (by the medium of) M. Marshall that the King of Naples has been recognized, and through him that he has just made a treaty which is yet secret, but which has all the force of a solemn treaty."[4]

With Bonaparte's second accession to power (and Louis's retreat from it) Marshall, it appears, became a covert spy for the monarchy in Bonaparte's camp. As Napoleon's second fall from grace approached, he requested Marshall's help to 'spirit' him from France. Sir Jonah Barrington, an Irish knight, spoke with Marshall after seeing the preparations that Marshall had been making for Napoleon's departure. "He proceeded to inform me that it was determined Napoleon should go to England; that he had himself agreed to it; and that (Napoleon) was to travel in Dr. Marshall's carriage, as his secretary, under the above mentioned passport. It was arranged that, at 12 o'clock that night the emperor with the Queen of Holland, were to be at Marshall's house, and to set off thence immediately; that on arriving in England he was forthwith to repair to London preceded by the letter to the Prince Regent, stating that he threw himself on the protection and generosity of the British nation and requested permission to reside there as a private individual."[5]

Marshall had worked out the plans carefully, but on the night of departure Bonaparte listened to the Queen of Holland and decided to stay, forever altering what might have been a different history.

Marshall wore, on special occasions, the title of Baron d'Avray of Ville d'Avray, (notwithstanding the fact that another family made claim to this honour since 1780), and his son Joseph was additionally created Chevalier de St. Louis as a result of Marshall's spy service.

Marshall lived the remainder of his life in relative obscurity, away from the public's attention. Aside from a duel, the wounds of which eventually killed him on January 9, 1838, Marshall was forgotten in the public records.

However in 1847, Earl Grey added a new chapter to this intriguing tale by personally recommending Marshall's son, Joseph, to Sir William Colebrook, Governor of New Brunswick, for the job of Superintendent of Education in New Brunswick.

Joseph was accepted for the job and in 1847 travelled to New Brunswick to form the Teacher's College.

The Marshall family continued to impact history for several generations that followed. In 1881, Loring Woart Bailey, Marshall's nephew, also moved to New Brunswick and the two families settled in the University's Old Arts Building. Loring Woart Bailey's son, Alfred Goldsworthy Bailey, studied at the University of New Brunswick (UNB) and eventually obtained his doctorate from the University of Toronto.

In 1938, Dr. Bailey persuaded the UNB and the provincial government to establish a history department, of which he was the only professor. When he arrived, Bailey found the worst university library in Canada and was so dismayed by it, he convinced Lord Beaverbrook to help. What resulted was like a literary Battle of Normandy. In a few short months, 50,000 essential books poured across the Atlantic.

For his years of dedication to learning, Alfred was named a fellow of the Royal Society of Canada and an Officer of the Order of Canada. His PhD thesis, "The Conflict of European and Eastern Algonkian Cultures", published in 1937, has been described as the first work of ethnohistory published in North America. During his lifetime, he published six books of poetry, including "Miramichi Lightning" which was shortlisted for the Governor Generals's Award in 1981 and he helped found "The Fiddlehead", one of Canada's pre-eminent literary magazines.

It was with that family history, under a crest that reads 'Nil desperando', that Arthur Bailey convinced his mother to invest in a tiny spit of land in the Okanagan.

# Chapter Ten Notes

1   Bailey, J.W., *The Curious Story of Dr. Marshall,* The Murray
    Printing Co., 1930
2   ibid
3   ibid
4   Archives of Foreign Affairs, France Vol 1801, Document 13,
    *The Bonaparte Papers*
5   Bailey, J.W., *The Curious Story of Dr. Marshall*, The Murray
    Printing Co., 1930

# CHAPTER ELEVEN
## GENESIS OF A LIFE-LONG DREAM

It took two years of wrangling on legal issues before B.C. Properties Ltd.'s proposal to the bankruptcy trustee was accepted and the company became the legal owner of 2900 acres at Fintry. At the time, B.C. Properties Ltd. was a family-owned development company and its shareholders were Mrs. (Helen) Ronald Graham and Arthur Bailey. In later years the company was owned entirely by Arthur and his wife Ingrid.

While the press incorrectly reported the property was purchased by Mrs. Graham, her involvement took the form of a loan to B.C. Properties Ltd., covered by a debenture. She continued to support the project with further loans which were

Katie passed away five years after she saw Fintry change hands to B.C. Properties Ltd., never having relinquished her hold on the Burnside house and property. It passed to her nephew, Roderick Stuart and was eventually sold to developers. *Photograph courtesy O'Keefe Historic Ranch archive.*

Art Bailey. His dream from the beginning was to make Fintry a showplace resort community. *Photograph courtesy B.C. Properties Ltd. collection.*

all retired over the course of time. While Mrs. Graham was involved with B.C. Properties Ltd., the driving force behind the company was her son, Arthur.

The negotiated purchase for Fintry required B.C. Properties to survey 300 half-acre lots and make them available to the people who bought building sites during the Fintry Estates Ltd. mail order sales period or who were in good standing and still paying off their mortgages on the $10 a month installment plan.

Graham Bailey, Arthur's son, vividly remembers the condition of Fintry when he and his brother Stewart spent their first night in the Manor House after the purchase in 1962, though he was only five and a half. They were assigned the benches next to the fireplace in the Trophy Room that first night. "It was pretty frightening. Bats were flying out of the fireplace and all these animal heads were above us and rats were running over the floor under our sleeping bags."

From the first summer visit with his boys, Arthur and his wife realized the enormity of the task they'd undertaken.

"The first time we arrived it was by boat and the grass was so tall Ingrid just disappeared when she walked across to the Manor House. It was like a wild jungle. Completely overgrown."

Some modifications to the property had been made from 1959 to 1961, including the tent camp" (campsite area now employed by BC Parks) Randall created during his short tenure as the General Manager for Fintry Estates Ltd., but it was clearly evident that no repairs to any of the buildings had been seriously undertaken.

Arthur maintained the Fintry Estates Ltd. offices in Vancouver, which were being managed by his controller Ernst Kaiser. From 1963 to 1969, Arthur commuted regularly to Fintry from his home in West Vancouver. His plan at the time was to include Fintry as one of the many projects he was managing, and to move there permanently when the de-

An aerial view of Fintry in the early 1970s. Note the fruit trees in the foreground compared to earlier shots of the delta. The last 200 trees were removed by B.C. Parks two decades later. *Photograph courtesy B.C. Properties Ltd. collection.*

velopment was underway. While Mrs. Graham travelled the world, spending winters in Nassau with company that included Sir Harry Oakes' family, Arthur began the process of subdividing the area for the 300 lots.

B.C. Properties Ltd. decided to provide the half-acre lots required by their purchase along what is now Muir Road, in an area adjacent to the Westside Road. Most of the lots were never occupied by their owners and some were put up for sale. Many remain today just as they were then, with "for sale" signs by various realtors sprouting along the gravel access road like mushrooms in the forest.

The decision to use the area above Westside Road was a pragmatic one. The development expense for the "300", including land surveys and road construction, was a cost B.C. Properties Ltd. would have to absorb. It was over and above the cost of the Fintry purchase price and could never be recovered. With half-acre lots, B.C. Properties was not required to provide water or power to the subdivided land. The directors of B.C. Properties Ltd. determined they might be able to ease the financial pain of that unrecoverable expense if they could quickly develop some prime waterfront lots on the south end of the delta.

From the beginning, Arthur saw the Fintry property as a resort club, with high-end homes nestled around a lush golf course, riding sta-

173

Arthur Bailey consistently dreamed of making Fintry a resort similar to the rendering pictured here. *Photograph courtesy B.C. Properties Ltd. collection.*

bles and tennis courts. He pictured the buyers as "club" members, owning a piece of the entire development in a fashion that would later become the norm in resort developments around the world. But for the present, like Dun-Waters who had to clear land to make room for his fruit trees, Arthur had his hands full logistically.

His first step towards development for the delta was to get water to flow again for irrigation and to supply the Manor House. The orchards were pruned and alfalfa was seeded in the pastures, but while the irrigation system built by Dun-Waters was still able to function, it was obvious that constant maintenance would be required. Over the years of neglect at Fintry, the wooden pipes and flumes located at the water catchment basin high up Shorts Creek had collapsed in several places. They were filled with sand and gravel. To make the system functional consistently required a process of laborious and time consuming digging and repair by hand. Wooden pipes had to be replaced with thousands of feet of aluminum. Suspension bridges had to be rebuilt. The catch basin had to be repaired and updated. And, even when that was done, the system had to be flushed repeatedly. Years of neglect had taken their toll. Arthur decided to use the old water system for irrigation and Manor House only. The lots to be developed on the delta would require a modern utility with a cistern, potable water piping and reliable service.

Because of the additional expense that would have been involved in replacing the "old" for "new" on the rest of the property however, the people doing the work and putting up all the money still had to make do with Dun-Water's turn-of-the-century wooden sluices. Ingrid, mindful of the dangers of contamination, began a habit of boiling domestic water at the Manor. It became a regular daily habit that still persists even though now it is unnecessary.

The Baileys, in spite of their wealth, often found themselves living like the earliest settlers on the delta. "It seemed like years before we got it working consistently," Arthur recalls. During the interrupted service periods, Stewart and Graham were employed hauling lake water at .25 cents a bucket.

"We'd have water for a while and then nothing. We'd have to go searching the system foot by foot to find out where it had failed. It was pretty clear to me the whole thing needed to be upgraded."

With the issues of water supply to the south delta more-or-less solved, Bailey now had to address the problem of power. It was still being generated by the original DC-power Pelton Wheel that Dun-Waters had installed. Pumping equipment that operated on DC current wasn't readily available. None of the modern conveniences in the Manor House would function on DC current either.

As the Pelton Wheel system was also wholly inadequate for an increase in the number of users that Arthur ultimately envisioned for the property, B.C. Properties Ltd. was forced to install their own diesel power generators and convert to alternating current.

With Gene Conroy, a man who had helped power the village of Banford on Vancouver Island, Bailey installed poles and had the wires strung. "We bought some of his used equipment, which was still expensive, to build our system here."

While it was a logistical nightmare, the task was quickly completed. Arthur realized how fortunate Fintry was to have Shorts Creek, just as Shorts and Dun-Waters had concluded before him and he suspected that Shorts Creek could be the source of more than enough power to meet the demands of future development. He decided to commission Interior Engineering to complete a feasibility study. Their assignment was to determine if it would be possible for Arthur to build his own dam on Short's Creek, install turbines and supply the power he would need. His idea was to construct a small dam in a narrow notch of rock above the location where the staircase to the waterfall now ends. The engineers determined it was entirely feasible.

"It would have only cost us $35,000 at that time. We almost did it, but B.C. Hydro agreed that if we would give them 13 hook-ups guaranteed for three years they would bring in power down the road. It wasn't cheap but it was cheaper than building our own system and we figured

175

we'd end up spending a lot of money on maintenance anyway."

The expense to B.C. Properties for Fintry was already climbing to beyond a million dollars and not a square inch had yet been sold. Cost of clearing the debts and the confused titles from previous owners of the $795 lots came to a staggering $565,000. Roads to the lakefront built by contractors like Cliff Serwa, alone clocked in at $70,000. There was the cost of the power, the water utility repairs and of course the original purchase price. Belatedly, Bailey was beginning to understand how Dun-Waters had pumped so much of his own capital into Fintry. He knew that somehow he had to begin squeezing income from Fintry or his dream would eventually bankrupt him personally and B.C. Properties Ltd. corporately.

In spite of the costs however, he never doubted his dream. When at Fintry in those early years, Arthur would often rise at dawn and walk the property alone. Each day brought him a fresh view of the future, a future he could almost taste, a future he felt destined to make happen. He saw manicured fairways and beautiful homes with their flowerbeds dressing the hillside in color.

With the water and power problems solved for the development, Arthur went to work trying to re-establish the area as the desirable resort of his imaginings. To begin, he undertook a road trip of media interviews across the West and in November 1965 he started the promotional effort.

"These facilities are to be expanded," he told reporters in Calgary, "to include a spa with swimming pool, a full-scale marina for boats and float planes, tennis courts and golf course, stables and riding trails.

"A partial re-subdivision has been carried out, and 50 paid-up purchasers of lots under the 1959 scheme have received title to new interior lots, along with options on waterfront lots. Others who are still paying on lots they bought under the original scheme will be granted similar titles and options as soon as they have completed their payments," Arthur told the press."[1]

To new buyers, Arthur tried to sell waterfront lots at the south end of the delta, priced from $6,000 to $8,000. He offered lots inland on the delta for $3,800 to $4,500 each.

"Our interest never diminished," Arthur now recalls. "Right from the day we bought the property we thought it should have been a destination resort and we worked towards that goal but we were just too far ahead of our time."

The Canadian market wasn't ready to emulate California in the mid-60s and Arthur learned that the hard way. His development plan, though wonderful in concept, was simply not believed with the memories of the Fintry Estates Ltd. debacle still fresh in the minds of prospects. Despite the career credits for upscale developments in Vancouver, even though Arthur was sincere in his descriptions of the future at Fintry, he was unable to command a starting price of more than $2,500 for the waterfront lots. That was a disappointment but also a burden financially, seriously hobbling his progress.

Part of the problem for the sales strategy was site access. The other was convincing banks that mortgages for land at Fintry were a safe risk.

Arthur recalls how lending institutions in Kelowna and Vernon simply refused to lend to prospective purchasers, claiming the development wasn't within their operating area. It made no practical sense, but that didn't seem to matter to the bankers. He also remembers how when interested parties arrived in Kelowna, they were often heartily discouraged by locals from attempting the drive up the treacherous Westside Road to Fintry. It was as if none of the cards were falling his way.

"They were very difficult sales to get people out here on that terrible, terrible road. It was just gravel and mud with two ruts. You didn't need to steer. You just got the car in the track and pushed the pedal."

"We had a Westside Road Committee that met once a month down on Nahun at the Dayton's house. There weren't that many residents on this side of the lake then, but there was Ron France, myself, the Daytons and I guess about eight or 10 others. We'd meet and we'd be writing letters to all the ministers and to the premier begging to have that road paved."

Over a period of years, the group invited every politician of influence they could find out to Fintry.

"We had Wesley Black out here, Gaglardi, Graham Lee. I think we had everyone of them (highway ministers) and we even coaxed Brian MacIver out. I said 'you know if you'd come out and promise some road improvement you'd get all the votes out here'. Well he did and it went NDP that year!"

Arthur fondly recalls the trials of trying to sell a development with goat trail access. "We would have people come to see us and stop at Nahun to telephone and say 'the wife won't go any further'. The women would often be hysterical. We'd have to go down by boat and pick them up."

Still, in spite of all the negative publicity, by November 1965, Arthur reported that he had sold 38 lots and began to acquire a small cash flow.

In 1965, B.C. Properties hired the husband and wife team of Wilf and Marge Potter to manage what was to become the renewed agricultural enterprise at Fintry (they remained managers of the ranch for 25 years, living in the "gate house" located at the entry to what is now the Park). They were perfectly suited to life on the still fairly isolated Fintry property and aside from Wilf's dreaded daily chore of crossing the canyon suspension bridges to clean the water intake basin of debris, they both took to the place like it always been their home.

To maximize revenue opportunities to be gained from the Potter's experience with animal husbandry, and to begin building the "resort" atmosphere Arthur felt was required to attract purchasers, B.C. Properties Ltd. decided to re-introduce animals to Fintry.

Helen Graham, wanting to get more actively involved in the rebuilding efforts at Fintry, took on that particular task with her own style and flare.

Dressed in her finest French designer outfits, draped in jewels and driven by a chauffeur, Mrs. Graham 'hit the stalls'. Accompanied by Wilf potter, whose job it was to point out the best animals, she regularly ventured from the Manor House to the Valley Auction Mart. Her appearances at the livestock pens must have raised a few eyebrows because Helen always looked as though she should be visiting Sotheby's rather than a saw-dust covered corral. Nonetheless, standing shoulder to shoulder with the ranchers and farmers in their dungerees, her toy poodle (dyed purple as a surprise birthday gift by Arthur) bundled under her arm, she bid on the livestock that Fintry needed. Pigs were eventually found for the sty, horses for the barn, chickens for the yard and cows for the pasture land.

Understanding it was the "attraction" that was more important to the plans for development at Fintry than the animals themselves, Arthur also contracted an American designer familiar with 'free range' animal zoos, to plan a children's park. Ingrid added peacocks, swans and geese to the menagerie. In a matter of a few months, Fintry went from unoccupied silence to noisy agricultural activity.

"We weren't raising the animals for sale or anything except for turkeys. We used them for meat and eggs. Most of the rest, the horses, pigs and cows became pets. A few years later, when we had the marina operating, the boys would paint the sides of the sows with advertising. It was that fun, quirky atmosphere we were after."

While Mrs. Graham populated the barns and stys with animals, Ingrid applied her own energies to the family project.

Mrs. Graham had decided to close the Graham estate house in Banff and transferred furnishings from there, from Mrs. Graham's house in Vancouver and from Arthur's West Vancouver home, out to Fintry.

178

Manor House rooms were turned into private guest rooms for Mrs. Graham's maids and visiting friends that included opera divas, artists, writers and politicians. The bunkhouses were converted into motel units for tourists.

Much of the organizational and operational effort at that time fell to Ingrid. Born in Salzburg, Austria her business background had prepared her for the challenge. She had worked with her step-father in the china and silver import/export business and worked in the ski resort and hotel business in Kitzbuhel.

When inspite of all the renovating and opening the extra rooms to visitors some of the furniture was still left wanting for space, Ingrid, displayed her ingenuity. She turned the furniture being held in storage into an antique store she called the "Bargain Barn", recruiting Marge Potter as the sales clerk.

Under Ingrid's direction, the campground was cleared and expanded and regularly filled by locals from Vernon and Kelowna. Day in and out, Ingrid saw to the meals of guests, to the linen changing, even to check-ins and outs at the campground. While she had some help in the kitchen, she handled the rest of the work herself exhibiting a Germanic penchant for efficiency.

She worked through a strict daily routine of tasks tirelessly and with a smile. To Ingrid's mind, assisting her husband's "work" in this manner came naturally. She seemed able to slip from housemaid to hostess with seamless ease, lavishing her European charm and grace upon guests as though it was her only duty. In truth, the opposite was the reality. Ingrid would have to rise before dawn to make breakfasts. She retired only after the last guest had called it a day, her only respite a quiet half-hour she might steal to eat her lunch aboard a row boat that she discreetly moved out of earshot on the lake.

Through it all, Ingrid refused to 'dress down', even when the work she had to do was menial. The sight of her at the pig barns, mucking stalls in her fringed white cowboy boots and jewels, often brought a smile to passing visitors but that too was part of the charm of the reborn estate.

With "attractions" in place, Arthur hired Vernon P.R. man, Vic Binnie, to initiate an active round of promotion for Fintry. It included an annual Fishing Derby that gained anglers' interest across the province. Television personalities like outdoorsman Keith McColl were as likely to be dropping a line into the lake off Short's Point as were local children. The Vernon and Kelowna newspapers published photos of the year's 'lunker' with the same enthusiasm displayed for international awards.

Art also commissioned Bruno Engler, the man who photographed the avalanche scenes in '*White Wilderness*' for Walt Disney, to produce a 16-mm promotional movie of Fintry

By stint on their dogged persistence, Fintry had become the biggest tourist attraction between Vernon and Kelowna and in 1966, Arthur thought he saw his first window of opportunity to cash in.

On February 4, the BC government announced the Strata Titles Act was to become effective that September. Taking quick advantage that June, with an architectural model of hillside condos borrowed from developers at Whistler, B.C. Properties announced two new development concepts for Fintry that would become a future norm elsewhere in the Valley. The first was 'strata title'. The other was the development of land in clusters.[2]

Mrs. Graham, once again decked out in her French designer hat and pearls, posed for the local media as Arthur described the new future for Fintry.

The development Arthur described would consist of "hillside villas" which were to be a modest one-and-a-half storeys high and have 600 square feet in floor space. Each would be carpeted, Arthur proudly declared, and equipped with major appliances. The asking price was also modest at only $10,500.

"We are basically in the land business," Arthur told the press. "We are inviting participation in a marina, clubhouse, model dude ranch and a shopping centre."[3]

Arthur, as the managing director of B.C. Properties Ltd., told the media the development would feature an 'escalift' to carry happy residents from the upper bench of the property down to beach and marina level. He had in mind San Francisco-style 'people mover'. His was a scheme whereby Short's Creek would be used to power an elevator with a water-wheel. For some arcane reason, it didn't occur to the local press to ask about Arthur's 'escalift' and he prudently kept the outlandish specifics of the contraption's design to himself. Instead, he emphasized plans to build the first 50 of the shake-roofed, expandable, attached hillside houses immediately. They would be open for inspection by the end of that summer he boldly declared.

In actuality, Arthur had two "show homes" built. Despite the reasonable price offered however, buyers for more were impossible to find.

"We tried everything but again, we were just too far ahead of the times." Arthur tried offering the strata titles at $1.85 per day for seven years; he offered a lease to purchase at only $58 per month; he even promoted cash discounts, but there were still no takers.

One of the "show homes" was moved to the delta where it still

This architectural rendering illustrates Arthur's vision of his 'hillside villas'. Note the 'escalift' structure . Arthur went as far as having a Vernon engineering firm complete preliminary designs of the water-powered mechanism. *Photograph courtesy B.C. Properties Ltd. collection.*

serves as a home, the other was moved to Silver Star Mountain to be used as a ski chalet. That experience told Arthur he needed to increase the lure of Fintry even more before buyers would line up for land.

It meant "making sure things were happening all the time", he recalls. To promote the area as a destination, in May 1966 B.C. Properties launched what Arthur planned as an annual fete at Fintry. He organized a "Kiddie Ranch" with stables, entered advertising floats in local parades and announced the first 'Festival at Fintry' for the May 24 weekend.

"The program, under the direction of Mr. A.W. Bailey of B.C. Properties Ltd., ranged all the way from horse racing to fishing on the lake. Dance music was provided by the Eldorados, a roast suckling pig turned on the outdoor spit under Cap Capozzi's capable direction," the local press reported of the first event.[4]

To add some glitz, Helen Graham invited friends and business associates from around the world including writer Johanne Stemo. The

An early *Fintry Queen,* still sporting the ferry loading ramp. *Photograph courtesy B.C. Properties Ltd. collection.*

The *Fintry Queen,* ready for her maiden voyage. To achieve the look of an old-style river boat took the Baileys many years and hundreds of thousands of dollars. The paddlewheel on the vessel's stern went through three versions before a workable , though only cosmetic version was constructed. *Photograph courtesy B.C. Properties Ltd. collection.*

gliterrati arrived by boat and plane from as far away as Beverly Hills just to join in the festivities. As a humourous side note to the party, the local press reported spotting Richard Burton and Elizabeth Taylor touring the property and Arthur, with a promoter's instincts, did nothing to dissuade the media from their error.

It was a terrific party, but the event did little to entice property investors. To get visitors to come to Fintry, B.C. Properties Ltd. still had to overcome the problem of distance from Kelowna and the dreaded Westside Road.

After nearly a quarter-million was invested in the ferry, the Fintry Queen was ready for her christening. *Photograph courtesy B.C. Properties Ltd. collection.*

Arthur decided to look to the water. In Vernon, he found the answer in the *Lequime*, an out-of-service gas barge that had once shuttled cars and passengers to and from Kelowna and Okanagan Lake's westside before the Kelowna Floating Bridge was built in 1956.

With his mother and Ingrid, he discussed the prospect of converting the skow to a passenger vessel that could be used to help sell the development. Everyone agreed it was precisely what Fintry needed, something that might reflect the tradition of past water transport on the lake and also be attractive to tourists. Most of all, with such a boat, Westside Road would become less of an issue to buyers.

Arthur invested in a naval architect's design for a paddlewheeler and the work began. At the outset, he now admits, he had no idea the project would end up costing him another $350,000!

Forty shipwrights were hired from the coast and moved into tents at the Manor House. Ingrid accepted the task of feeding the men while Arthur waded through the government red tape.

"Trying to convince the government to certify the boat was a nightmare. We had to take the whole thing apart, right down to the propellers and shafts on the hull, then start over again," Arthur remembers.[5]

"When we first bought the boat my brother and I were assigned to the cleaning of the bilges below deck, mucking out with shovels," Graham Bailey says.

"We had an older cousin named Bob White. He was about 14 when he first started coming to Fintry in the summers about 1963. He was sort of our straw boss. Everyday we had about four hours of things to do."

Arthur made use of the entire family to create the *M.V. Fintry Queen*. Gradually, level by level the ferry was converted to its present state. The first incarnation though had the boat without a top deck covering. To protect his passengers during inclement weather, Arthur used his imagination to creatively solve a problem. Umbrellas would have been an easy answer but they were too expensive. Instead, when the skies opened during a cruise, he gave his passengers a complimentary $2 plastic raincoats from a consignment that he'd purchased at the Army & Navy Store in Vancouver. He applied the same creativity when it came to dealing with the provincial government liquor licencing authorities. In order to be permitted to serve alcohol aboard, the *M.V. Fintry Queen* had to be designated an 'oceangoing ship'. To gain that rating it had to carry mail between 'ports of call'.

Arthur pragmatically had Fintry postcards printed and began to send them to his friends in other cities. "We might have carried one piece of mail at a time, but we did it," he says[6]

"At that time, about 1967, we bought a barge and a tugboat from the CPR in Penticton. We used the barge as a breakwater for the marina that had some 100 slips. On the barge we were going to put some tennis courts but we never got around to that." They added a gasoline barge, some rental boats and a small tackle store. Arthur assigned his sons to management of the new Fintry enterprise which was additionally an attraction for prospective lot purchasers. For the summer months, Graham would manage the marina and Stewart, a year older, would serve on the crew of the *M.V. Fintry Queen*.

The evolution of the *M.V. Fintry Queen* involved topside additions made as money was available. Arthur learned about naval construction as he went along. The stern paddlewheel, for example, went through two early failures.

Graham remembers spending a week painting the first version in every imaginable color of the rainbow. When Stewart and Graham had finished the paint job on the first paddlewheel, everyone gathered on the shore to take pictures of the first 'sea trials'.

"The very first turn the boat made twisted the stern paddlewheel into

Graham Bailey (seated) and Stewart Bailey survey their handiwork after painting the Fintry Queen. *Photograph courtesy B.C. Properties Ltd. collection.*

nothing. Bits and pieces were floating everywhere about 500 yards off the Fintry dock. I remember my grandmother (Helen Graham) yelling to all the crew to jump in the lake and try to salvage the pieces."

Graham thought it was the expense that concerned his grandmother but Arthur knows better. "It wasn't the money. She just didn't want anyone to know where all that scrap wood had come from!"

For a time, the *Fintry Queen's* stern was left unadorned, but after two years a second version was put in place.

"By then we had put a housing on that was quite a bit leeward of where it currently extends. We put the first of the salon area on there. The paddlewheel was working great. We had lots of runs with it between the Westside ferry dock and Fintry.

"Then one day the Rotary was having a charter. The men were on the back deck happily referring to the paddlewheel, talking about the cruise and how nice an occasion it all was to be out on the lake in a paddlewheeler. As they talked, the thing made this awful noise, broke off and just disappeared out of view. It dropped somewhere off of Manhattan Point in about 250 ft of water."

Helen Graham and Cap Capozzi enjoy a joke during the first cruise of the Fintry Queen. *Photograph courtesy B.C. Properties Ltd. collection.*

That time the cause wasn't faulty design.

"We learned that our engineer on the boat couldn't swim. He was in charge of greasing the pillow block bearing on the paddlewheel and after years of operation, those bearings had never been greased because he was afraid of climbing out over the water. It just seized. Insurance wouldn't cover the loss because it was determined to be our engineer's negligence."

Marvin Hagloff, a local diver, made an attempt to locate the expensive structure and did so, 250 feet down. When Arthur and the diver returned to salvage it however, Hagloff was unable to relocate the paddlewheel in the lake's murky depths.

And it wasn't just the paddlewheel that fell from the *M.V. Fintry Queen*.

Proud of the vessel, and mindful of safety, Arthur invested thousands of dollars to purchase a retired Navy anchor with 10 tons of chain. The anchor assembly was skookum, so hefty in fact that captain of the vessel at the time refused to take the anchor aboard for fear it might sink

The Fintry Queen, sans topsides later added, became a modern symbol of good times in the Okanagan to tourists the world over. *Photograph courtesy B.C. Properties Ltd. collection.*

the boat. When he finally relented, the *M.V. Fintry Queen* was motored to her moorage and the anchor dropped over the side amid cheers and clapping.

Unfortunately, no one had thought to secure the bitter end of the chain.

"We thought when the anchor hit bottom that the chain would stop, but it kept on going. We watched in horror as every damn link of chain slipped over the side and there was nothing we could do about it," says Arthur.

Wiser, but undeterred by the loss, Arthur decided to use a buoy and an old Caterpillar tread as an anchor. As Graham had gained his scuba diving license, he and Gerry Lenz, a retired Air Force mechanic Arthur had hired to maintain equipment at Fintry, were given the task of affixing chain to the tread from a buoy located off the beach at Fintry.

The young man and the experienced diver took the assignment in stride. The tread had been dropped about 55 feet below the surface and rested on a ledge near a deep precipice in the lake bottom. Lenz loaded up with a heavy belt of tools and rapidly dropped to the tread.

"We had lots of visibility and plenty of stability standing on the tread," Graham recalls, "but for some reason when we got down there

Gerry took his flippers off and handed them to me. We fed the chain through the tread and linked it to the buoy. He was working, holding this chain with one hand and the wrench in the other and he leaned backwards. The tools on his belt swung and he just fell off the tread. He went over the edge of that precipice in the blink of an eye. He was dropping from sight and he didn't have his fins on."

Graham reacted immediately, diving into the darkness after the older man. "That was the scariest thing I ever had to do in diving. I had to chase this guy over the edge and he was falling, falling, falling out of site with all this weight attached to him and no flippers to swim against it. He was absolutely frozen in panic. I caught him and got rid of his belt and when we got back up there was a big argument about who was going to pay for all his tools!"

Neither Graham or Lenz did much lake diving after that.

With a functioning tour boat that was regularly taking prospects from Kelowna to Fintry, Arthur had solved part of his problem, but then he realized he needed to offer the guests more reasons to make the journey.

Imbued by the prospects of success with the tour boat and the marina, Arthur turned to providing entertainment for the visitors once the boat docked at Short's Point.

With the packing house handy, he decided to create a friendly restaurant and pub.

"To qualify for the liquor license we had to count every room we had. We had to call the bunkhouses we'd turned into a sort of motel, 'satellite' rooms. It was a stretch but the inspectors went along part way. I think because we were trying so hard to make something out of Fintry," says Arthur.

Before the formal approval of a pub license, visitors were all sold 'memberships' when they arrived. No one seemed to mind. The pub operated through the week during the summer months. Bands were imported for special evenings. They showed movies. They held dance contests. Arthur was open to almost any activity that might generate activity at Fintry and provide him with an opportunity to talk business with prospective lot buyers.

Though Arthur had worked diligently at trying to erase the $795 lot sales approach from the public memory, in 1968 glaring headlines brought it all back to haunt him again in an indirect way.

On January 12th, Sid McDonald's battered body was found in a blood-stained station wagon on a North Burnaby street. Preliminary reports stated Sid had been shot in the head, but latter examinations proved this to be false. The Vancouver promoter had been beaten.[7]

The Packinghouse converted into a pub/restaurant became the centre of social life on the Westside Road for years. It was two storeys, featured an elevator and cool room for fruit storage. One summer, streakers became as regular a sight as Arthur and Ingrid bustling about attending to visitors. *Photograph courtesy B.C. Properties Ltd. collection.*

Under the glare of the media, an intense police investigation soon uncovered their suspicions that Sid had been murdered in home nearby. The night after his body was discovered, eight members of Satan's Angels, a Burnaby motorcycle gang, were brought in for questioning. Police determined that blood matching Sid's type were found splattered across a television set that had been in the gang's clubhouse.

Quickly, Robert David James, a 24 year-old biker, was arrested and charged with non-capital murder. During the trial, a witness testified that she had seen James bludgeoning the promoter in the gang's headquarters.

In the flurry of front page reports on the murder, the press uncovered snippets of information on McDonald's business history including his most recent involvements with a multi-million dollar hotel development in Point Roberts, Washington. McDonald's partner in that business was financier Arnold Swanson, the former squire of England's Notley Abbey, who was serving time in prison on a morals conviction at the time of Sid's death.

Though separated from Sid for two years, the death came as a blow to his wife, Wendy. It was the third time tragedy had struck her life. In 1950, her first husband, R.A.S. MacPherson had died in a light plane crash off Point Roberts. Wendy assumed the presidency of his company, B.C. Bearing Engineers and continued to operate the firm.

In 1954, she married William Derek Dix, a vice-president with Neon Products of Western Canada. In 1957 Dix disappeared in a boating accident that also claimed the life of Patrick Cromie, the assistant publisher of the *Vancouver Sun*.

The press reminded the public of McDonald's land scheme at Fintry, calling him "one of the backers of a plan to cut the 2,500-acre Fintry Estate on Lake Okanagan into lots and sell them by mail order." [8]

Bailey shunned the press's requests for comment on his former friend, preferring to focus all his attention on the bright future for the property. In February he donated a lot at Fintry to the Vancouver Home Show as a promotional stunt, he hosted Ski-Doo dealers to a reception at Fintry and he curried whatever favor he might from his growing political connections.

In August 1969, Arthur volunteered to host the 17th Social Credit Party anniversary party at Fintry. While generous, his offer was not completely altruistic. Bailey knew the political coverage would publicize Fintry and the more publicity he could get, the better his chances for the future sales.

The Bailey family spent weeks in preparation. The octagonal barn was to become party central and serve as a casino, so Stewart and Graham were assigned the renovations.

"The family always felt a huge value in that barn," says Graham. "We wanted to put our own animals in there. It was just a wonderful structure. When the Fairbridge Farms School left the property, it had been badly maintained. There was an awful need to clean it up. In the barn we had to dig up hardened manure with pick axes.. We literally had to chop it out. There were beautiful concrete floors under there but we thought we were walking on earthen floors. It was a month and a half of digging before we realized that."

On the day of the party the 250 Socred guests, were ferried to the property from Vernon aboard the *M.V. Fintry Queen* and met by young women in grass skirts.

"Champagne corks popped amid flickering patio lights," the newspapers reported, and Arthur served up roasted pig like a traditional Hawaiian as ministers of the government chatted about election strategies. [9]

Notables at the party included Pat Jordan, Leslie Peterson, P.A. Gaglardi, Donald Brothers, Bill Vander Zalm and Bill Bennett. As Arthur expected, attendees also included the media, and key among them was Socred-bashing columnist Allan Fotheringham.

Fotheringham, in a rush to ridicule the gathering for his newspaper, compared the event to the annual Excursion Day of the Knights of Pythias in Stephen Leacock's *Sunshine Sketches*, and failed to properly recognize the history surrounding him at Fintry. All of Bailey's effort to focus media attention on his

Former B.C. Premier Bill Bennett and Ingrid. *Photograph courtesy B.C. Properties Ltd. collection.*

jewel were dashed with a few paragraphs of ridicule by the noted columnist.

Describing the property the day after the event, he wrote: "Fintry was a fenced kingdom with a staff of 80. It was also, 10 years ago, the bait of real estate crooks who sold 3,000 "waterfront" lots to unsuspecting Prairie buyers - who found the lots were 1,000 feet up the mountain."[10]

Fotheringham chose to ignore the massive investment that B.C. Properties Ltd. had made to refurbish the property, or to credit those involved with its rebirth. Helen Graham, it should be noted, had tried to maintain the Dun-Waters 'feel' at the Manor House by adding hundreds of thousands of dollars worth of private treasures from her own sojourns around the world to the decor.

In his report however, Fotheringham described the decor in the Manor House as gauche. He enumerated the fixtures as being "Hollywood decor circa 1938. A touch of Gloria Swanson in the wilderness."

While the columnist dashed Bailey's hopes for some promotion of Fintry further afield than the Okanagan, it did nothing to deter his efforts to garner sales. By 1970, the *M.V. Fintry Queen* was running regularly with its stern paddlewheel secure, the tent camp was operating, the marina and the pub were all going concerns. Bailey hired Baron Albrecht von Gadenstedt, who had been the owner-manager of Adventure Bay Resort in the 1960s, as the general manager at Fintry. Von Gadenstedt was responsible for all the facilities at the development itself including the 240-acre tent and trailer park, the picnic grounds, marina, dining room and dance parlour, beer parlour, motel, lodge and stables.

Jack Cooper, of Kelowna, was charged with responsibility for the *M.V. Fintry Queen* and Arthur continued his efforts with real estate subdivision development.

Progress on the lot sales was slow, but the tourist business at Fintry generated enough revenue to keep the effort alive. Motorist magazines such as B.C. Motorist and Chevron USA had discovered the tourism show at Fintry and colorfully described the star of the performance: the *M.V. Fintry Queen*.

It was because of that growing fame among the motoring tourist market that Arthur received a proposal, the first of several, to make Fintry an 'exclusive' way-station for particular groups. Members of the Church of Jesus Christ of Latter-Day Saints offered to purchase Fintry and turn it into a club for campers. Arthur rejected their appeals. American developers came closer to getting his commitment for sale until they let slip that their plans called for the demolition of the Manor House. He also turned down a proposal to lease the property as a camp for an American trailer club whose members owned Airstream Trailers.

"It would have been lucrative. They wanted to lease it for 10 years and make pads for a thousand trailers. I turned them down flat too." To Arthur it seemed such uses were a desecration of the property. Besides, he had a better offer percolating.

A company that had been instrumental in developments at Lake Tahoe decided they would like to purchase Fintry. Arthur believed the one thing he didn't have that could make his dream for a resort development at Fintry come true, was cash. The company, Cal Pacific Inc., had lots of it. In 1973, B.C. Properties agreed to enter into a joint venture with Cal Pacific.

"The plan was to develop the property like a resort which is what we had in mind from the beginning. We were still trying to sell lots on the south delta to pay for the improvements we were making.

"At the same time we were building the resort side of Fintry with the *M.V. Fintry Queen*, the marina and the pub. We'd already put several hundred thousand into the *M.V. Fintry Queen* and I still needed more money to put the salon on. Cal Pacific

192

agreed with me about the golf course and the resort development concept, so we worked out a share arrangement where they would put up the money for the development and we'd share the profits at the back end. They also agreed to pay for the last bit of work on the *M.V. Fintry Queen*."

Throughout his life, Arthur had done business based on faith. He assumed honesty and integrity in his business partners. From the day he decided to sell to Cal Pacific however, that faith was tested again and again. Cal Pacific borrowed their investment cash from the Bank of Montreal, using the property to secure the loan but Arthur had never considered that Cal Pacific might not share his ever-present vision for the property.

With Cal Pacific's borrowed money, work on the *M.V. Fintry Queen* was completed. The tourism draw of the property was a bright as ever. The provincial government announced that they were finally going to pave the Westside Road. Everything looked perfect for the future and Arthur initiated serious planning for the resort development that was to be undertaken.

But unbeknownst to Arthur, Cal Pacific was getting cold feet. The investors hadn't counted on the red tape they'd encounter in trying to get Fintry approved for development. Seeing time pass with interminable meetings, a decade of past frustration by Arthur in his attempts to get government approvals and little progress being made towards completion of their plans this time around, Cal Pacific finally decided to walk from their deal with B.C. Properties Ltd. in 1976.

That decision, Arthur realized only much later, was the beginning of a nightmare which was to last for more than two decades of his life.

# Chapter Eleven Notes

1  Calgary Herald, November 23, 1965
2  Vancouver Province Wednesday June 22, 1966, p 16
3  Vancouver Province June 22, 1966
4  The Daily Courier May 25, 1966
5  The Daily Courier, February 23, 1992, p A3
6  The Daily Courier February 23, 1992 p A3
7  Vancouver Sun, Jan 12, 1968, p 1
8  Vancouver Sun, Jan 13, 1968 p 2
9  Vernon News, August 4, 1969
10 Vancouver Sun, Tuesday, August 5, 1969

# CHAPTER TWELVE
## A B.C. PARK IS BORN

Arthur and his American partners had big plans for Fintry.

They included a marina resort club, golf course, tennis facility, commercial area, a dude ranch with stables and bridle paths tent and trailer park. Their plan was to make Fintry as popular as Lake Tahoe to the wealthy in search of recreation.

When Cal Pacific decided to withdraw however, it put all that future Fintry development on hold. To maintain the B.C. Properties grip on their investment, the company was forced to service a total of $800,000 in loans undertaken by Cal Pacific with the Bank of Montreal (reduced by approximately $225,000 by B.C. Properties ltd. through land sales before the debt was completely retired).

In May 1976, Arthur announced that Fintry was for sale with a price tag of $3.6 million in order to regain some of the money owing the bank. Arthur told the press that the possibility existed for Fintry to be turned into a recreational club. B.C. Properties Ltd.'s intention was to pay the bank by creating the club. Bailey told the media "the club is in the process of being incorporated and it would have exclusive rights to use the land."[1]

The announcement included modifications to the plans that Cal Pacific and B.C. Properties Ltd. had for the property and folded in the lot sales he had already made on the delta in the 'bigger scheme'.

"Included in the proposed development of the private resort would be an 18-hole golf course and tennis courts.

The plan was well thought out but it didn't develop soon enough to pay the bank, which decided to foreclose.

Ken Johnstone.
*Photograph courtesy*
*B.C. Properties Ltd.*
*collection.*

Bailey arranged to borrow $880,218 from Lancer Financial Ltd., enough to pay off the Bank of Montreal debt and have some cash left over for development. While Ken Johnstone's company's loan commanded 30% interest, compounded monthly, it was an option Arthur thought he could manage temporarily.

"When B.C. Properties went to court in Vancouver with financier Ken Johnstone to confirm we had the funds to pay the Bank of Montreal, we discovered the Province of British Columbia had an offer to purchase Fintry before the courts. Strangely, the press were there with their story about the purchase all ready for release," Arthur states.

"The court decided to accept B.C. Properties' offer of settlement to retire the bank although an accounting was necessary as the bank couldn't confirm the outstanding balance."

It took a few months for the bank's accounting to be completed, during which time the previously mentioned property was sold to reduce the debt. By October 1976, Bailey had repaid the Bank of Montreal their outstanding loan of $574,000. With that issue resolved he began to focus attention on the development again and went back to the press.

"The once-rumored private club proposed for Fintry Estates on Westside Road has become a reality," the newspapers reported. "Sod has been turned, signifying the first stage of a golf course, and plans in the offing include a dude ranch, marina, platform tennis and tennis courts. The once-public and popular camping site has been taken over by its former owners, B.C. Properties Ltd. and an association has been formed to perpetuate the private club."[2]

In actuality, no sod-turning ceremony had been conducted as was reported. In fact, B.C. Properties Ltd. was still farming at Fintry as usual.

Bailey told the press that the association mentioned would be buying two major blocks of Fintry Holdings with memberships expected to go from $2,500 to $3,000 each. He said the public would be able to use the golf course on specified days and have access to the marina.

To raise more capital for the development and to help pay down the debt to Lancer Financial, B.C. Properties also began selling land. The High Farm, up to that time the least likely parcel of Fintry to be developed anyway, became a cash resource. By August of 1977, chunks of the property totaling 350 acres, D.L. 3333, 3803 and 4693, were sold to Sir Christopher Oakes, Barr (grandson of Sir Harry Oakes of Nassau) and his artist wife, Julie Cowan, for $146,752. Mrs. Graham had been friends with Lady Oakes for some time and Arthur had assisted Chris and Julie on several occasions: offering them the use of 'The Chalet' as a home; assisting Julie to open an art school and gallery in the granary building on the property; and, helping Chris by offering the horse stable and corral for a riding school he proposed.

In June 1978, the mortgage agreement with Lancer Financial was modified to $934,422.

Bailey's effort seemed to be paying off. Finally, after 15 years, Bailey thought he could see his resort concept realized. That October, the Central Okanagan Regional District directors finally voted to enter a land use contract with B.C. Properties Ltd. "for a development that will include a 200 unit strata motel, a nine-hole golf course, tennis courts and an upgrading of existing facilities on the Fintry delta.

"The total area being considered for development is about 560 acres and subsequent stages may include a 200-unit condominium hilltop resort and a 75-unit guest ranch."[3]

Again, press reports were slightly inaccurate. B.C. Properties had in fact proposed a 200-unit strata condominium development and a marina hotel.

Bailey is quoted in one newspaper as saying the development idea was the same one initially proposed for Fintry a decade and a half earlier "but government red tape and changing the ground rules every two years has held up plans,"[4]

On September 17th, 1980 Lancer Financial decided to foreclose. Despite his friendship with Arthur Bailey, impatience was winning out with Johnstone when it came to the development of Fintry.

Arthur sought investors, managing to hold off the Lancer foreclosure by one week with a payment of 10 housing lots in the Kaslo area and promises that a sale of Fintry was in the offing. Arthur and Ingrid had three offers to purchase Fintry on the table: one from Klaus Linemayr, of Vernon; another from a group led by Lawrence Salloum, of Kelowna; and, a third from an Edmonton group led by Peter Pocklington.

Klaus Linemayr, a Vernon land promoter with his own partners, the West Coast Credit Union, seemed to be the best. Bailey thought he'd finally found a monied partner who shared his dreams for Fintry and with whom he could honestly deal.

On May 13th, B.C. Properties Ltd. accepted a $3.65-million offer for Fintry from Linemayr. A sum of $2.2-million was paid in cash but the extension on foreclosure by Lancer had been expensive. On the closing of the deal with Linemayr, Bailey turned over $1,744,573 to Lancer. The rescue loan and top up from Ken Johnstone in 1978 cost B.C. Properties dearly. While it may seem unbelievable viewed from today's regulated financial point-of-view, Bailey was forced to pay back nearly twice what he'd borrowed in less than three years time. But he *had*, after all, accepted the terms so that he could hang on to Fintry and was legally bound by them. The sting of having to pay so much for the loan was soothed somewhat however. B.C. Properties Ltd. was still owed $1.45-million and two three-bedroom condos that were to have been built for them lakeside from the Linemayr sale.

Unfortunately, the agreement Arthur had accepted in good faith proved to be less than it appeared.

Bailey's original plan was to retire at Burnside. Linemayr put up money to make the down payment and offered part of the property at a higher price to his partner, West Coast. "After the Burnside house and property purchase there followed a meeting in Victoria with my solicitors, Linemayr and the West Coast Credit Union. We disagreed about the purchase price recorded for Burnside," he recalls.

The result was court and the beginning of several lawsuits between Linemayr and his financial partner, the West Coast Credit Union.

"To protect the interests of B.C. Properties, our solicitors had to file suit against both parties. In settlement we had our legal bills paid, a registered 25-year lease on the Burnside home and property, $160,000 for alterations and a registered option to purchase Fintry," Bailey says.

"It was my oversight on my part and my solicitor's to allow Linemayr and West Coast to subrogate development costs to my mortgage. They ran up $1-million in front of my mortgage in so called development costs."

In order to deal with the expense, Arthur and Ingrid began searching for an investor who would agree to purchase Fintry using B.C. Properties Ltd.'s option. While Ingrid travelled to meet prospects in Europe, Arthur discussed the future with Ken Johnstone and his wife Oli, a longtime friend of Ingrid's. Bailey alleges that together they agreed to an arrangement whereby Lancer Financial would buy the Fintry property providing Arthur would stay involved with the unfolding plans for development. Under the terms of their agreement, Arthur alleges that he was to service prospective development investors as well as attend to the engineering, Regional District submissions and property improvements. After completion of development and after Johnstone had recouped his investment, Bailey claims the verbal agreement stipulated that the two companies would share in the profit.

"So I accepted the approach by Lancer Financial a second time and we exercised my option," Bailey remembers.

By the time Ingrid returned with another possible investor ready to buy, the Lancer Financial Corporation Ltd. purchase was underway. The acquisition was for $2.2-million "on terms I believe were $200,000 down," says Bailey.

As it turned out, Johnstone had made a savvy deal. By February of 1989, Lancer began to receive down payments from other developers interested in participating at Fintry. Bailey, true to his word, acted as an intermediary between Lancer, architects, engineers, golf course designers and as many as 200 prospective investors. Although Bailey believed B.C. Properties Ltd. was entitled to receive a share of the down payments, Bailey saw none of that cash. By the end of 1989, Lancer received $270,895 in non-refundable deposits from such developers. In 1990 another $1,100,623 worth of non-refundable deposits were received. In total, Lancer banked $1,371,519 in deposits from interested developers on deals that were never completed, covering not only the cost of the financial corporation's initial down payment for the property but also paying for more than half of the purchase price.

Development strategies continued apace however, and Lancer sought government approvals for a new plan that called for 900 condominium units and 400 lodge and hotel rooms.[5]

All but final approval to an 80-hectare (200-acre) residential resort complex and 18-hole golf course at Fintry, designed by Golf Course Inc. of Canmore, was received from the Central Okanagan Regional District in July 1989.

"A proposed second phase of Fintry Estates to be built on hilly land (bench land) above the delta includes another golf course and 3,275 single- and multi-family housing units. Both phases of the project are to be built over the next decade. Upon completion of both phases of Fintry Estates, an estimated 15,000 new residents could be added to the area." [6]

Of greatest concern by the bureaucrats was the packaged sewage disposal system included in the proposal. It raised warning flags by the Sierra Club of Western Canada who screamed for full environmental impact statements. The plans were investigated and subsequently approved.

Some Fintry residents presented a 39-name petition to CORD protesting the development proposals, in spite of the fact that the potentials of development of Fintry were made clear to them from the beginning.[7]

Bailey continued to seek investors to purchase back Fintry and was repeatedly successful in finding them, but Lancer Financial, just as regularly, rejected their offers.

"First Mr. Johnstone asked for $5-million and then $9-million and then it was $12.5-million. When he was asking $9-million we brought him an offer from a Swiss firm for $7-million cash and he turned it down," says Arthur. When the price was up to $12.5-million Bailey brought Johnstone an offer from a Calgary group for $12.5-million on terms with a substantial amount down and the rest in Fannie Mae Bonds. Unfortunately, Arthur claims he was later told that the Bonds were unfamiliar to Johnstone's solicitors and therefore that offer was also turned down.

Contrary to the alleged agreement Bailey says he had with Lancer Financial, Johnstone's advisors were apparently working privately on a deal of their own, a deal to sell Fintry to the provincial government in partnership with the Central Okanagan Regional District, for $7.68-million. CORD, the group of elected officials and bureaucrats who had stymied development on so many occasions, would be contributing $2-million to the purchase price. Whether the parties involved were working secretly can be debated, however Bailey claims his alleged agreement with Johnston stipulated that both parties were to have made a full disclosure of any sale discussions as they were happening and Bailey was never informed of the government's interest. Ironically, while Bailey was attempting to orchestrate acquisition with his own investors, he was also servicing the many government officials who were apparently sent to Fintry to scope out the property before the purchase.

In late 1995, a gala was organized at Lake Okanagan Resort where the government announced that Fintry would become a park.

The local media reported that provincial Parks Minister Moe Sihota called the park at Fintry a once-in-a-lifetime opportunity 'since the land has been in private ownership for more than a century'.[8]

"This was quickly becoming a now-or-never proposition for our government," said Sihota.[9]

The Minister told the gathering that part of the government's decision was prompted by the fact that other offers for Fintry were being received and that the land might not have been available if they hadn't acted to buy when they did. Was he referring to the repeated approaches that Bailey had made to Lancer to buy back Fintry?

After the sale, serious legal differences erupted between B.C. Properties Ltd., Lancer Financial and the Baileys. The differences were defended through the tremendous unselfish assistance of the Bailey's close friends: Mrs. Robert Christensen, Willie Rometsch, Ross Fitzpatrick, Tomas Capozzi and Gordon Geddes. Through negotiations by Willie Rometsch, Oli Johnstone and Arthur, an out-of-court settlement was finally reached.

To the uninvolved observer, the entire sales process with its repeated rejections of offers that might have led to resort development at Fintry, seem to smack of subterfuge on the part of the players involved. Bailey continues to assert that he was never informed of the negotiations, which he claims was contrary to his verbal agreement with Johnstone. Then, after the sale, the manner in which the announcements of the purchase were made and the declarations that followed them were handled with callous disregard for the people who had struggled to keep Fintry viable. The fact that the government failed to acknowledge and recognize the contribution made over 35 years to maintain the Fintry Estate and ensure that future generations could enjoy the heritage structures that still remain there, is shameful in the least.

Arthur is the proud father of his two sons who were most helpful during the early years at Fintry. The oldest son, Stewart d'Avray Bailey, is currently vice-president of T.R. Communications Inc., San Francisco. He lives there with his wife Cynthia and their two sons, Malcolm and Ian. Arthur Graham Bailey is a senior consultant with the Investors Group in Kelowna where he resides with his wife Valerie and their sons Andrew, Patrick and Cameron.

Arthur and Ingrid continue to enjoy the beauty of Fintry in quiet seclusion at Burnside, where they intend to live until 2012.

As for the provincial park, the couple say they are pleased to know that the delta that so captured their hearts and brought them so much joy will continue to benefit British Columbians and visitors from around the world for generations to come.

# Chapter Twelve Notes

1    The Progress, May 19, 1976, p1
2    Kelowna Today, Oct. 7, 1976, p 11
3    Capital News, October 18, 1978, p 1
4    ibid
5    Daily Courier, July 11, 1989, p 1
6    ibid
7    Daily Courier, July 11, 1989, p 1
8    Daily Courier, Dec. 15, 1995
9    ibid